When you
come to
the end of
YOUR
ROPE
there is
HOPE

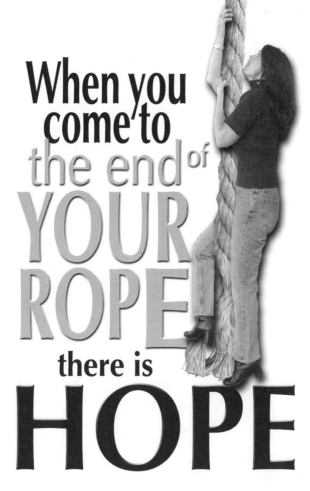

When you come to the end of YOUR ROPE there is HOPE

Phyllis Tomberg Giglio

SYNERGY Publishers
Gainesville, Florida 32614 USA

A division of Bridge-Logos International Trust
in partnership with **Bridge-Logos** *Publishers*

When You Come to the End of Your Rope There is Hope
by Phyllis Tomberg Giglio
© 2002 by Phyllis Tomberg Giglio. All rights reserved.

International Standard Book Number: 1-931727-00-7
Library of Congress Catalog Card Number: 2001095970

Published by:
Synergy Publishers
Gainesville, Florida USA
SP-7007 Inspiration
www.synergypublishers.com

Synergy Publishers is a division of Bridge-Logos International Trust, Inc., in partnership with Bridge-Logos Publishers.

Book Design by: Leader Design Group
                    Elizabethtown, PA 17022
                    717-367-7763
                    info@oneleader.org

DEDICATION

To my husband, Sal, our marriage has known balmy
breezes and hurricane force winds. God has steered us
safely through them all and the harbor is almost in
sight. Thank you for loving me for a lifetime.

ACKNOWLEDGMENTS

Thank you my Messiah, for showing me the reason to write this book. Your grace has indeed been more than sufficient!

Thank you, Mother. You left me too soon, but I feel your spirit in all I do that is worthwhile.

Thanks Dad, for all you taught me through the years. You were not only my natural father, but also my spiritual father. It was your persistent prayer that brought me to Yeshua.

Thank you Joe, for helping me through rough times. Your prayers meant more to me than you will ever know. Your faithfulness has been priceless.

Thank you Raphael, for your gentle prodding and encouragement to write. You believed I had something to say and prodded me to say it—and here it is!

Thank you, Dr. Sam Deets, for taking on the project of editing this book. Your patience and guidance have made it a reality. You have been a real friend.

Thank you, Mark Tomlin, for your expert proofreading. You made me look good. Thank you for sharing your enthusiasm for my story.

Thank you to all my family. You make my cup run over with joy.

Thank you Sister Elizabeth Simmat, for discipling and mentoring me. You passed the mantle on to me and I pray I have worn it worthily.

Thank you Sara, Elsie, Annette, Kitty and Judy for being more than friends. You are my beloved sisters.

Thank you to the folks at Bridge-Logos Publishers for sticking with me, especially Guy Morrell and Tracy Deken.

Foreword

Some might call her old-fashioned. Others might say she's a true survivor. Still others might believe she'd have to be a little crazy—after all, twelve kids in this world would leave anyone hassled and harried! But, after almost five decades of child rearing, six sons, six daughters, and a multitude of spiritual children "rise up and call her blessed."

This refreshing look at joyous family living—with a few kinks and quirks thrown in—proves that marriage and motherhood are still God's Plan A for many kingdom women.

Bright, witty, charming, and articulate, Phyllis writes a confessional of her own weaknesses, some tough tests, and God's infinite grace. This indomitable woman represents one of the last champions of solid family values. Or is she on the cutting edge of a brave new frontier? Either way, young moms and older ones will take courage, shed a few sympathetic tears, and enjoy some chuckles as they join Phyllis on her journey of **When You Come to the End of Your Rope There is Hope**.

— Anne Severance, former East Coast Acquisitions Editor
Zondervan Publishing Company

Table of Contents

CHAPTER I

The Journey Begins

inter cold bit my toes and my nose ran as I stood on that New York City sidewalk Christmas Eve, 1940. To a nine-year-old the myriad of twinkling colored lights shining through our neighbor's windows warmed me, in spite of the snow, ice, and frigid cold. Mesmerized by the sparkle of the reflected light from the tinsel decking the Christmas tree, I thought our street was transformed to a winter wonderland.

Having a vivid imagination, I loved pretending to belong to a different family living a different life. I imagined living inside the homey scenes I saw with my young mind's eye. Picturing a life beyond the lace curtained windows; I played a starring role. I joined the children gathered around the piano singing Christmas songs about a little babe born in Bethlehem.

Logs burned in the fireplace warming me. Glancing towards it, I smiled to see stockings, including mine had been hung on the mantle waiting to be filled by Santa. In the center of the room, a beautifully decorated Christmas tree dripped with garlands, lights, and decorations. Crowning the tree was a beautiful angel with gossamer wings. The delicious aroma of Christmas goodies wafting from the kitchen completed the image.

On that Christmas Eve, I imagined myself attending services with this family in their majestic stone church on the corner. I had never been inside the church, but I knew it would be both mysterious and beautiful. My parents warned me that we had to be very cautious of churches, because churchgoers would try to convert us. Still, I wanted Christmas, every part of it!

In reality I envied my friends as they anticipated and prepared for the wonder of their holiday. I didn't begrudge them their joy, but I felt so left out. Santa never came to our house with presents. How I wished he was unaware that we were Jewish!

My grandparents always told me that being Jewish was something very special. It meant I was one of God's chosen people. However, when the world was celebrating Christmas, I didn't think "being special" was so great. I wished I could be born again as a Christian child. The truth is I was ashamed of being Jewish.

Though I wished I were Christian, being Jewish did have some advantages. I enjoyed having extra days off from school for Jewish holidays. I enjoyed wearing my best clothes and going to the synagogue services. Relatives would visit and we would have special meals. My grandmother would cook all the traditional dishes, like homemade challah bread, crisp potato latkes, sweet raisin and spice-laden kuegle and, of course, her own gefilte fish.

Grandmother would start her famous gefilte fish recipe by buying a live carp that weighed in at about fifteen pounds. To keep it alive she would allow the carp to swim in the bathtub until she was ready to cook it. It was fun to visit her and see her makeshift aquarium—the carp's residence until he met his culinary fate.

I especially loved the Passover Seder and the story of God's deliverance of His people from their bondage in Egypt. We had a separate set of dishes, pots and utensils that were used only during Passover. At the Seder ceremony, we kids got to take part as the age-old story was retold about Moses and cruel Pharaoh, just as it had been told for centuries. But even in the midst of these treasured family traditions I longed for something more.

This is the story of my exodus out of a personal Egypt spanning more than the biblical forty years. As I press on towards the Promise Land, I know God has set my path and guided the journey from little Jewish girl to the woman I am today. I faced a childhood of dysfunction, lived as a harried homemaker for nearly five decades, and now share my life as an encouragement to women facing the challenges of life.

CHAPTER II

You Don't Have to be Crazy ... But it Helps!

Having twelve children is not very commonplace. When people hear that I have six sons and six daughters you can't imagine the comments and reactions! Once, at the hairdresser I heard a reaction I'll always remember. The lady in the next chair didn't know me, nor I her. She was reading an article to her hairdresser from the local newspaper about my candidacy for school board.

"Can you believe it! She has twelve kids!" she loudly exclaimed.

Her hairdresser's reply was accompanied by an exaggerated groan, "You'd have to be crazy to have twelve kids!" she proclaimed.

Well, I didn't want to answer to that, so I remained anonymous. But, I thought to myself, "You don't have to be crazy, but it helps."

I have always loved large families. When I was a little girl and saw a big, happy family I wished I could be part of it. I guess we should be careful what we wish for; I did become part of a big happy family—my own.

It seemed our house was the gathering place for all the neighborhood kids. Of course, most of them were mine. Their friends would knock at the door and ask, "Can anyone come out to play?" It didn't seem to matter which one, just "anyone."

They especially loved being invited to stay for dinner. When they saw our large table set for dinner, it looked as though we were having a party. One evening we had so many friends staying for dinner we ran out of forks. Much to my chagrin the kids creatively solved the problem among themselves. It was called, "Pass the Fork while You Chew."

People often ask, "How did you do it; where did you get the energy and money to raise twelve children?" The answer is, we could never have done it alone. By God's grace, we made it through. I always knew God loved my children even more than I did and He would equip me for the task. I believe He had more confidence in me than I had in myself. Although I was pregnant for nine years, they weren't consecutive years. I did get breaks between pregnancies. My maternity wardrobe, however, was worn much more than my "civilian" clothes.

I amassed some interesting statistics recently. I changed at least 28,000 diapers and tied 20,000 pairs of shoes. I don't know how many times I stuffed toddlers into leggings and sweaters, zippered up their jackets, tied their scarves, pulled on their mittens, only to hear, "I gotta go potty." I prepared at least 50,000 meals. I couldn't begin to calculate how many loads of laundry I did, but I outlasted five washers and six dryers. Like the famous battery bunny, "I am still going."

To get an idea how many twelve children are, they are enough for two basketball teams plus two officials; or a baseball team, plus three pinch hitters; and too many kids for one pew in church. Now that our family includes daughters and sons-in-law and grandkids, we have grown to fifty. We can just about fill a Greyhound bus.

My kids did, by and large, reap the benefits of a big happy family, albeit a dysfunctional one, like most American families. I once saw a magazine cartoon that showed a huge auditorium with a banner over the stage that read, "Annual Meeting of Functional Families in America." Seated in the audience were two people.

CHAPTER III

Meet My Parents

orn on June 21, 1931, I grew up thinking it was so special to be born on the longest day of the year because my birthday seemed to last longer. My parents were Saul Tomberg, an ex-U.S. Marine whose parents emigrated from Austria, and Celia Orenstein, whose parents emigrated from Russia.

Both families came to the United States in the early 1900s to escape the persecution of the Jews in their respective native countries. The play, *Fiddler On the Roof*, vividly captures the experience of the European and Russian Jews who were forced to leave their beloved homelands. Families left behind all that was familiar to face the arduous trip across the Atlantic to an uncertain new life. They fled with their hopes and their dreams and little else hoping to find a safe haven in America.

When I was eleven months old my mother died of pneumonia. In 1931 there were no antibiotics to fight virulent infections and because my mother was overweight, her heart gave out. She simply could not fight the disease that claimed her life. I can remember hearing someone say, "Celia only became heavy after the baby." I was that baby.

Those idly spoken words left an indelible impression on me. For most of my life I subconsciously believed I had caused my mother's death. It wasn't until much later when my life fell apart and I was seeing a counselor that I realized I had been bearing this tremendous guilt, along with a great fear of abandonment.

All I know of my mother is that which was told to me. Relatives said she was intelligent and sweet, and loved me very much. The only picture I have of her shows a pretty, plump, fashionably dressed young woman. Beside me in a baby carriage, she is standing with my tall, handsome dad. I was probably nine months old. She looked so pleased and proud. She could not have known she wouldn't live to see me reach my first birthday.

After her death, my mother's folks wanted me to live with them so they could care for me. My dad didn't want to give me up because I was all he had left. So, to provide a home for me he asked his mother to find him a wife. Marriages were often arranged in those days. He married Gertrude, a pretty young woman from a good family. She had been hoping to find a husband. He barely knew her and really didn't love her. He was merely looking for someone to make a home and care for me. Predictably, this proved to be a poor basis for a happy marriage.

When they married they made an agreement with my grandparents, telling them they would be allowed to visit me provided they kept the truth of my real mother a secret. Since I was only a baby when she died everyone assumed I had no memory of her. In my heart, yet, I have the memory of a very special someone who cared for me and loved me and then suddenly was gone.

To make matters worse, my father was an alcoholic. This is an unusual problem among Jewish men, but he was, indeed, addicted. I don't know if it was genetic—two of his brothers drank heavily—or if it was because of my mother's untimely death, or perhaps because of his hard life as a Marine for five years.

I can remember his coming home from work, getting angry, and pulling the tablecloth off the table that had been set for dinner. Food, dishes and angry words would fly. Screaming arguments were a nightly occurrence. I would hide under the bed or in a closet with my hands tightly covering my ears to shut out the sounds of tumult. I felt it was somehow my fault that they fought. I would wait until things got quiet and then would come out and try to be a peacemaker. I would go to my dad and ask him to be nice to Mommy. Then I would go to Mommy and tell her Daddy didn't mean it. Unfortunately, nothing I did helped. Sometimes I think having my large family was a subconscious effort to create the happy family I didn't have as a child.

Amid the unhappy times I do have some wonderful memories of my childhood. I can remember a lot of fun things my dad and I did together. When I was eight years old he took me to the 1939 World's Fair, which was held in Queens, New York. It was exciting to see exhibitions from other countries and displays of how life would be in the future.

My dad took me to the annual Macy's Parade that used to be held on the day after Thanksgiving. He would put me on his shoulders so I could see over the crowd. I loved the marching bands, and I would clap as the drum majors threw their batons high in the air. I would cheer as Santa Claus with his toy-laden sleigh and his reindeer would pass by on a snowy float that looked as if it had just arrived from the North Pole. Every year I hoped he would come to my house.

I can remember summer Sundays when we would take the subway to Coney Island. I had so much fun splashing in the waves. With my dad's help I would build elaborate sandcastles with turrets and moats at the water's edge. Afterwards we would ride the big Ferris wheel on the boardwalk. Its name, *WONDER WHEEL*, was written in bright lights. When we reached the top, I thought I could see the world. But, back on the ground, I saw the reality of the frequent stops at the many beer gardens.

My dad and stepmother subsequently had four children. The drinking and arguing escalated. With the addition of four younger siblings, however, I didn't blame myself as much for their fighting. I enjoyed being a big sister to my three brothers, Stan, Mel, and David, and to my sister, Sandra. There is a strong bond between us and when we get together today we are all like kids again though we are each past fifty years of age.

My dad was seldom home to help in raising the children. He worked long hours in the clothing factory he owned in Hoboken, New Jersey. He also lived a life apart from his family. He took separate vacations, continuing to drink heavily. My stepmother was understandably hurt and unhappy with the way he treated her.

Looking back I can see she often redirected her anger for him toward me. It seemed she thought everything I did was wrong. When they divorced after thirty-two years of marriage, she told me I was the cause of all her troubles and the reason my dad married her and caused her so much pain. As an adult I can understand how she felt, but as a child I was hurt by the way she treated me.

CHAPTER **IV**

The Truth Comes Out

The summer I was twelve, quite by accident, I found out about my real mother. The saying, "Sooner or later the truth will come out," proved true.

I grew up thinking the two people whom I called Grandma and Grandpa were just a wonderful elderly couple who favored me above my siblings. I once asked my parents why I called them Grandma and Grandpa and why my brothers and sister didn't. I was told they had taken a liking to me when I was a baby and we lived next door to them. I was told they had no grandchildren and asked me to call them Grandma and Grandpa. After we moved, I was told they wanted to keep in touch with me. They would come to see me every couple weeks and bring me presents. I thought it was great. Kind of like having a real-life fairy godmother and godfather!

During a weekend visit to their home I tore a page out of a book that, unbeknownst to me, belonged to my mother. Grandmother became very upset and slapped my hand. I angrily retorted, "You can't hit me; you are nothing to me!"

"Nothing to you!" she exclaimed.

11

She then told me to get my grandfather who was working in the garden. They proceeded to tell me about my birth mother. The conspiracy that kept me from knowing the truth ended.

This brought a lot of peace to my grandparents, who naturally had always wanted me to know about my mother. But, finding out the truth about my birth mother made me feel very insecure. It was as though the foundation of my life had crumbled. It was hard to believe that I was lied to all this time. I felt as though I could never trust grownups again. I felt as though my life was shattered into little fragments. My stepmother was enraged. She felt betrayed by my grandparents and forbade them to come to our home or visit me ever again. Every chance I got I would run away from home and go to my grandparent's house.

I developed an even more loving relationship with my grandparents now that I knew they were my real mother's parents. I got to know my own family. My mother had younger brothers who had families of their own. I met my two cousins, Beverly and Francine. I also got to know my maternal great-grandparents.

My great grandfather was a taciturn, intellectual man, who read constantly. This was very exasperating to his wife because she wanted him to pay more attention to her. My great grandmother was a fiery redheaded little woman who freely spoke her mind.

There is a story told of her being critically ill later in her life and she was seemingly on her deathbed. All the family was gathered around her. She motioned for her husband, Yonkel, to come closer to her. He lovingly bent down close to her. She beckoned him to come closer still. It was a very poignant moment. In her weakened voice, she said, "There is something I have to tell you." Great grandfather tried to reassure her that it was all right and not to tax her waning energies by speaking. "Please listen to me, she insisted, I have something I must say."

"All right my darling, what is it?" he whispered.

"Yonkel," she said, "you have not been a very good husband."

Great grandmother recovered, but I am not sure their relationship ever did. These were the relatives who taught me the fundamentals of relationships!

Meanwhile, the more time I spent with my grandparents, the more my stepmother's anger toward my grandparents increased. It created a great breech between us that did not end until my first child was born. We were constantly at odds with each other. It didn't help that I was precocious and thought I knew it all. I refused to take correction from her. The growing animosity between us made our home a battlefield. We had many screaming matches that sometimes escalated into awful physical clashes.

CHAPTER V

The Wisdom of Bubeh

My dad knew something had to be done to defuse the situation between my stepmother and me, but he did not know what to do. He finally turned to his own mother, Deborah, for whom he had a great love and respect. She was the wise family matriarch, not unlike Deborah in the Old Testament. To me she was my Bubeh, which is Yiddish for grandma.

Her family often turned to her for advice, so Dad brought our family problem to his mother. She advised, "Saul, you should buy a farm and raise your family in the country!"

Bubeh thought this would remove him from the big city entice-ments that kept him away from home. Living the life of a farmer would force him to be more involved with his family. At the time, this suggestion seemed absurd to my dad. He owned a factory that made ladies' coats. He was a "citified" New Yorker. He loved his fast lifestyle of wine, women, and song. What did he know about farm-ing? But, when things went from bad to worse between my step-mother and me, he reconsidered Bubeh's suggestion.

"I have a cousin." This expression was used a lot among the immigrants who came to this country from Europe. A cousin could be a relative or someone that came from the same town you did. Actually, my dad did have a cousin. He owned a chicken farm in Lakewood, New Jersey. Dad contacted him and was invited to go spend time learning about chicken and egg farming. He spent three weeks with him. During that time his cousin also helped him find a farm he could afford. When he returned to the city, Dad announced that he had bought a farm in Hightstown, New Jersey.

We kids were excited at the prospect of moving to a farm with live chickens, cows, and goats. My stepmother didn't share our enthusiasm. She liked living in the city where she had the support of her family that lived nearby. However, my dad finally persuaded her that this move would give them a brand new start and a better life. He promised her she could go back to the city for visits with her family any time she wanted. It took a lot of convincing, but she eventually agreed, and we headed for the farm and our new life.

The ramshackle appearance of the old farmhouse on the outskirts of Hightstown did nothing to convince my stepmother she had made the right decision. The house needed major repairs. The barns were nearly falling down. The only decent building was the chicken coop. So, my dad decided to start his farming career right away by raising chickens.

Soon we became acquainted with our neighbors, the Estenes, kind and loving Christians who took us under their wing. A family who had earned their livelihood as farmers for many generations, they became our main source of farming information and our guardian angels. They walked my dad through the elementary things he needed to learn, from milking a cow to planting crops.

I think the elder Estenes are reaping many heavenly rewards because of their kindness toward us. They not only taught us about farm life, they also gave us food when we had none. I have fond memories of their son Henry. He was like a big brother to me. Late at night we would use flashlights to secretly send Morse code messages to each other from our bedroom windows. He also watched out for me in school and tried to keep me out of trouble.

16

My dad was a quick learner and a hard worker, but he must have raised some eyebrows among the local folks. He could be seen hoeing the crops and feeding the chickens wearing the monogrammed silk shirts and tailored slacks that were remnants of his former life. He didn't own overalls because he didn't have any extra money with which to buy them. So, he made do with what he had.

The little money he earned on the farm was spent on equipment and seed. Farm work is strenuous and winter or summer, there are always more chores to be done than there are hours in the day. Because I was the oldest of five kids, I became the main source of farm help. My dad and I used a two-man saw to cut up many old barn beams to burn in our furnace for heat. Coal cost money, but the beams from dilapidated barns were free!

Every morning before school I would milk our cow, Daisy. On cold winter mornings it felt good to lean against her warm body to stave off the cold winds whistling through the cracks in the walls. In the summer I was often smacked in the face by her tail as she slapped away at buzzing flies. After school, there were eggs to collect, clean, and pack for market. In the summer we kids would weed or harvest the crops. On the weekends my brother Stan and I worked together cleaning out the hen houses.

Stan has a wonderful sense of humor and a quick wit. Often as kids on the farm, we laughed more than we worked. One Saturday as Stan and I scooped up shovel after shovel of chicken manure, I thought out loud, "I wonder if this will give me muscles?"

His quick reply was, "If you eat enough of it, it will."

Another time my stepmother came home from the general store and said a man there told her to drink a glass of Pepsi Cola after dinner to heal her frequent heartburn. My dad asked her if the man was a doctor. "No," Stan interjected, "he was the Pepsi salesman."

He still makes me laugh when we get together for family reunions and we recall stories of the old days on the farm. We reminisce about the good times and the hard work. We remember a gravel pit on the farm where we often played. We called it "Magnificent Valley." We recall the indescribable flavor of fresh-picked sweet corn and the taste of juicy, warm watermelons we broke open and ate while still on the vine.

I worked hard on the farm, but I really didn't mind. Somehow my dad made us believe it was a privilege to work with him. If you sulked or gave him the idea there was something else you would rather be doing, you could lose this privilege. I think the biggest benefit of farm life was that my dad really got to know his children and teach them things only a father can teach. We worked together and played together. Bubeh had advised her son well.

CHAPTER VI

The War Years

Dad still drank, but not as much, since there were not as many opportunities to carouse. So, he was home with us most nights. For amusement we gathered around the dome-shaped Philco radio to hear our favorite programs. *The Shadow*, *The Lone Ranger*, and *Easy Aces* were among them.

Everyone had to be very quiet when Dad listened to *Gabriel Heatter and The News* each evening at seven o'clock. Our country was in the midst of World War II and Dad was anxious to learn all he could. Three of my uncles were fighting overseas.

We eagerly looked forward to receiving V-Mail from them. These letters were written on regulation parchment, thin, blue paper that was letter and envelope all in one. Each letter was censored before it reached us, lest a military secret would be disclosed. A popular slogan in those days was, "A slip of the lip can sink a ship."

Everyone was involved in the war effort, civilian and military alike. Women worked in defense plants that made planes and munitions. It was the era of "Rosie the Riveter." She was a poster girl, her hair in a scarf and her sleeves rolled up to reveal muscles. She represented these women. Some who had perhaps never worked outside their homes replaced the able-bodied men that were serving in the military.

Older men volunteered as air raid wardens. They were to take charge in case we came under air attack by the enemy. Signs marked "Air Raid Shelter" appeared everywhere there seemed to be a safe location. We were trained to go to these marked areas in case the bombs fell.

During the war years everything from gasoline to candy bars was in short supply. We learned to conserve and save. When I left food on my plate at dinner I was admonished that children were starving in Europe, so how could I dare leave food on my plate? Somehow that never made sense to me. First, how could what I ate affect starving children halfway around the world? Second, if they were indeed starving, why didn't we send them the leftovers? We saved newspapers, tin cans, foil wrappings and cooking grease, all of which was collected and recycled

This is when margarine became popular as a substitute for butter and saccharin was used as a substitute for sugar. The government said that butter and sugar were needed for the war effort. I guessed they were some kind of secret weapons.

Nylon stockings became the substitute for silk stockings. I tried to imagine why our soldiers on the battlefield needed silk stockings. Much later I learned that the silk threads that stockings were made of were used to make parachutes!

In order to insure that everyone would get a fair share of necessary items, each family member was issued a book of ration stamps by the government. These stamps were needed in order to purchase everything, including shoes. Families would often barter gas stamps for food stamps as needs arose.

People didn't mind the hardship of doing without because it was for the war effort and the boys fighting on the battlefront. It was a time of patriotism and cooperation—everyone working toward the same goals. Someone once said, "If you could have a wartime mentality in peace times, you would have an ideal society."

Meanwhile, the Tomberg war raged with no sense of cooperation or common goals. My stepmother and I fought constantly as I
entered the teen years. Living on the farm did not bring a resolution
to the animosity between us.

Chapter VII

Rebellion

started dating before I was fourteen. I was physically mature for my age and easily passed for eighteen. I dated indiscriminately. My rebellion made the situation worse at home, and I took every opportunity I could to get out of the house. Soon, I was cutting classes and missing school. I didn't care whom I dated, just as long as I went out. I even dated older men. I later found out that one was married. I became promiscuous. For some reason, I didn't know how to say "no." I don't know if I feared rejection or just craved acceptance.

I started experimenting with alcohol. I knew what I was doing was wrong, but I was in real rebellion. One night, on a dare, I drank a pint of brandy. I woke up the next day with no memory of the night before. There were other things that I did that I wish I could forget. I put myself in dangerous situations with people I had no business being with. I thought I was in control and lucky because I remained unscathed by my reckless lifestyle. I ran away from home the summer I turned fifteen.

I felt the allure of Asbury Park long before Bruce Springsteen immortalized that seashore town in his songs. I lied about my age and was able to get a job waiting on tables in a fancy Asbury Park hotel. Room and board was provided for the hotel workers so I had a place to stay. I was finally free, on my own, and loving it! My folks didn't know where I was until I called them. I was glad they didn't force me to come home. I'm sure the house was much more peaceful without me.

Those were the glory days of Asbury Park, New Jersey. In the 1940s and 1950s it was a prime vacation spot along the shoreline. The beach and boardwalk were wonderful. Frozen custard, lemonade, hot dog stands, and games of chance lined the crowded boardwalk. The delicious aroma of food combined with the noise and music coming from the booths created an intoxicating atmosphere that was the sights and sounds of summer. At the end of the boardwalk stood "Tillie." She was a round, wooden building that housed the best merry-go-round in the world. What fun it was to hold tightly to the leather reins and reach out far enough to catch the brass ring without falling off my painted horse as I swept by.

The weekends were the best part of all. My friends and I would hurry to Convention Hall on the boardwalk as soon as we finished work. We danced to the music of the Big Band era. Benny Goodman and Jimmy Dorsey were the rage. We danced into the wee hours of morning. As long as I did my work at the hotel I was free to do what I wanted when I wanted to do it. It was probably the most exciting and fun-filled summer of my life. I loved my newly-found independence. I loved feeling in control of my life.

Sadly, when summer was over I had to go home. It was a hard transition. Having tasted freedom and life on my own, I rebelled against all restrictions and curfews. I began to hang out with an older crowd of kids. We smoked, drank and thought we were having the time of our lives. I thought I was lucky to have friends and freedom to live, without being harmed by my folly and indiscretions. But as I look back, it wasn't luck at all. I can see that all the time the Lord was watching over me, protecting me. Years later when my own children rebelled during their teen years, I sadly realized the apple doesn't fall far from the tree.

Chapter VIII

Saturday Nights

Hightstown was a typical small town. The only exciting place to hang out was the Candy Kitchen. If you have seen the soda fountain on the *Happy Days* TV show, you know just what the Candy Kitchen looked like, jukebox and all. Everyone went there after school. The cool kids had their own booth and I was one of the cool gang.

Having money to spend for clothes and to go places was very important to me, so I had a series of after-school jobs that paid about thirty-five cents an hour. The job I enjoyed most was working at the Candy Kitchen. I could hang out with my friends and get paid. It was especially cool, because I could give my friends free refills on their sodas.

Most Saturday nights my two best friends and I would dress in our crinolines, poodle skirts, and saddle shoes and take the bus from Hightstown to Trenton. The dances held at the Trenton Moose Club were the place to be for young people from miles around. I loved to dance and it was fun to have different dancing partners each week.

One Saturday night after the dance, my friends and I visited a brand new restaurant back in Hightstown, Giglio's Tomato Pies.

This was the first pizza place in our rural community. Though some of the people in town thought tomato pie was a two-crust pie filled with tomatoes, it didn't take long for them to acquire a taste for this Italian specialty.

Chapter IX

Singing Sal Makes the Scene

W e entered the new pizza place and took a table. A good-looking guy with a ruddy complexion and light brown hair combed in the popular, pompadour style came to our table and introduced himself. He said his name was Sal Giglio and he was the owner of the place. I wasn't too interested in him because I had a boyfriend. However, my girlfriends were. They thought he was sharp and very good-looking.

We told him we lived in the country and were waiting for a ride home. He said he was closing in fifteen minutes and would be glad to take us. I called my dad and told him a very nice guy that owned the new pizza restaurant was going to drive us home and he did not need to come for us. It was a very cold night, so I think Dad liked that.

When Sal closed the restaurant, we piled into his car. It was a 1937 Oldsmobile, one of the big ones. I was impressed, because the guys I dated drove pickup trucks. Sal took my two friends home and then me. He parked in the driveway with the car running and heater on, and we talked for a couple of hours.

Sal told me he was twenty-two. He had lived in Brooklyn all his life and at eighteen he was drafted into the Army. In a short time he

27

became a Corporal, then Sergeant First Class. After infantry basic training he went to radio school to be a high-speed radio operator. He described the three and a half adventure-filled years he was stationed in Europe. He shared his life ambition to be a singer. I was impressed to learn that when the war ended and he came home, he had the opportunity to go to the prestigious Julliard School of Music in New York City.

His family, like many others, had been hard hit during the depression of the late 1920s and early 1930s, and they often did not have money for the simplest needs like food and clothing. Because of this he developed a strong work ethic. Getting a job and earning money was top priority for him, so he declined the offer to attend Julliard and opted to join the work force. I have often wondered if he regretted lying aside that opportunity.

I also learned he had been working since he was a young boy. It was not unusual for people of that generation to go to work at a young age. This was the generation that Tom Brokaw referred to in his bestseller, *The Greatest Generation*[1]. They went to work early in life because their families needed the extra income for food, clothing and rent. During the Depression when there were no jobs, the whole family would work together to survive.

As a youth, Sal would shine shoes on subway trains to supplement the family income. He soon learned he could make more money by singing on the trains. He would check his shoeshine box in a subway locker and sing for the passengers. After he sang, he would pass his hat around and collect coins from his appreciative audience. Some days he would earn more than his father did.

Panhandling was against the law. Once, he was arrested and sent to a juvenile home for ten days. He should have, instead, been commended for wanting to help his family. When I think of the awful things that happen in subways today I am reminded how times have changed.

As Sal and I sat in my driveway and he told me about his singing ambitions, I asked him if he would sing a song for me. He did. The song was *I'll Never Smile Again*. I was hooked. What a voice! He was a wonderful singer in the crooner style of Frank Sinatra. But as far as I was concerned, Sal sounded better.

I told him a little about myself. I said I was eighteen though I was only fifteen. I was so used to lying about my age and using a fake ID to get into bars, I almost believed I was eighteen. He asked if he could see me again.

I said, "Yes."

Little did I know that that evening would change the course of my life forever!

CHAPTER X

The Tapestry

ecently I thought about the probability of Sal and I ever meeting. The chances were very slim. He was an Italian Catholic from Brooklyn, New York, with connections to the Mafia; I was a Jewish farmer's daughter from Hightstown, New Jersey. Our backgrounds were so totally different there had to be a divine plan involved. Or, as they say in Yiddish, it was *Bershert*, or "meant to be."

Some might say it was fate. Others might say it was kismet. I say God had a plan in mind. He took the diverse strands of our lives and wove them together creating a sublime tapestry. In this life I can only see the back of the fabric, which is a jumble of unmatched threads, stitches and knots. Someday, however, when time ends, on the other side of eternity, I will see a beautiful combination of colors and textures combined in the marvelous tapestry that God fashioned from our lives.

The circumstances that brought us together were unique. During the war years when Sal and his brother Al were in the Army, his dad and mom left their Brooklyn apartment to move to

Hightstown to manage a large country estate that was owned by a relative who was a Mafia boss.

When the boys were discharged from the Army after the war, their parents prepared to move back to their home in Brooklyn, New York. During these three years, however, Sal's Mom and Dad had become very valuable to "Uncle Joe," as Sal called him. He begged them to stay and continue working for him; he made them an offer they couldn't refuse.

Typical of Mafia operations, he said he would set up a pizza restaurant in Hightstown for the boys. He would own it, but "on the books" it would belong to Sal and his brother Al. The family agreed to give it a try.

A building was purchased, renovated and equipped to be a pizza restaurant. Al was a baker by trade and he became "the pizza man." Sal was the manager and waiter. Within a couple months, however, Al wanted out. He was engaged to a girl back in Brooklyn, and he decided he couldn't live so far from his beloved. So he left Sal with the entire responsibility.

Sal had to learn how to make pizza, while maintaining his role as manager and headwaiter. He took some lessons from an expert pizza maker in Trenton, New Jersey, and soon had those pizzas twirling high in the air. People said Sal's pizzas were the best they had ever tasted. I worked as a waitress for him after school and on weekends. We dated for the next four months. If we weren't spending our evenings together, we would have long schmaltzy telephone conversations. I was falling head over heels in love. He told me he felt the same way.

In the forties, love story magazines were very popular. *My True Story* and *True Confessions* were considered risqué. Because I was told not to read them I, of course, read them all. Between the covers of those magazines I found stories of romance, intrigue and unrequited love. I was especially caught up in the tales of young teenagers running off to marry. A seed was planted. I decided I would do it, too.

I was desperate to leave my home where the battles still raged between my stepmother and me. I desperately wanted to be in control of my life. This was the root of my rebellion. Growing up in a dysfunctional, alcoholic environment, I had very little control over the events in my life. I was never sure what would happen next. Added to the formula were the scars from the knowledge of my birth mother's death and the awful relationship with my stepmother.

These things made me feel that life was unpredictable. I was very vulnerable. It seemed to me the only way I could protect myself from being hurt was by taking control of my own life without any parental interference. Getting married would provide that opportunity. Ours would be what some psychologists would call a typical "jailbreak marriage."

Sal and I had casually talked about someday marrying, as lovers often do. When I approached him with the idea of actually doing it, he didn't object. He had become disenchanted with working the many hours a week that running a restaurant single-handedly required. We were young and in love, so the idea of eloping sounded very romantic.

I knew my parents would never permit me to marry at such a young age, so I didn't even broach the subject to them. Sal's situation was different. He felt obligated to tell his uncle, the real owner of the restaurant, that he was leaving. Uncle Joe did not take it well. He ranted and raved and said, "No one is allowed to quit on me!"

But the die was cast and our plan to elope grew more and more attractive. Sal's uncle was very angry, to say the least, and would not give him his last two weeks' pay. I didn't have any money either. Sal discovered eighty dollars in nickels in the jukebox. And with that money we began our life together.

We took off for Elkton, Maryland, to be married because they didn't require parental permission. I don't know how I learned this. It may have been information I read in those same romance magazines.

So, Maryland was our destination as we embarked on the sea of matrimony.

Chapter XI

Two Become One

I still hadn't told Sal my real age and he didn't suspect I was only fifteen. I knew I had to tell him, but I waited until we were halfway to Maryland. I began by telling him I wasn't really eighteen.

"Are you seventeen?" he asked.

"No," I replied, "I am fifteen."

He became pale, and panicked! I thought he would turn his "Merry Oldsmobile" around and dump me on my doorstep, but he didn't. I'm sure it crossed his mind. However, we continued on our way to Maryland. On February 10, 1947, we were married by a justice of the peace.

We pledged our lives and love to each other "for better or for worse, for richer or poorer as long as we both shall live." We had no idea what those vows would mean. That night we felt happy and secure in our decision to spend the rest of our lives together.

When we called our parents and told them we were married they didn't share our joy. Both sets were angry. My dad was angry because I was so young, and to him it seemed that I was throwing my life away. Sal's mother was angry because I was Jewish. In those

35

days, marrying out of your religion and nationality caused as much scandal as marrying out of your own race did.

When my uncles heard the news of my marriage to a "goy" they persuaded my maternal grandparents to take me out of their will. Prejudice is nothing new. It has been around as long as there has been a diversity of people. We had made our bed and now we were literally lying in it.

On our wedding day, we returned to Long Island where Sal began working as a pizza baker. We spent our honeymoon night in a room over the bar and grill where Sal worked. It was not, by any stretch of imagination, a honeymoon suite. But, we were in love and nothing could dim our joy. It seemed like a five-star hotel to us. The flashing neon lights of the sign that read, "Arty's Windmill," added a special ambiance. Music played in the background. It came from the jukebox in the bar downstairs. The song, "Peg O' My Heart" repeated over and over and over.

Memories are peculiar things. I may not remember what I had for lunch today, but I will never forget Arty's Windmill and "Peg O' My Heart." I couldn't have been happier. I was now Mrs. Salvatore Giglio, a married lady.

CHAPTER XII

Famiglia

*S*al's mother and father had emigrated from Palermo, Sicily, to America. His three older siblings were very young when their parents brought them on the ship, *The Tantaglare*. It was not an easy journey, for the family had to make the long trip below deck in steerage class. Most of these passengers became seasick. It was crowded and had very little ventilation.

When the Statue of Liberty was finally in view, everyone rushed on deck and let out a tremendous cheer because they had arrived safely. After living under Fascist rule with mandatory military service, Sal's father, like many others aboard ship, longed for a life where his sons wouldn't be forced to fight in wars. At that time, the United States was a neutral country. He also sought a better life for his family. Even if the streets were not made of gold as had been rumored, he felt there would be more economic opportunities for his family in this country.

The first time I met the family was at the wedding of Sal's brother, Al, two weeks after our wedding. When I was first introduced to them, I thought Sal had fourteen sisters and brothers instead of the seven he had told me about. It seemed each one had an American name and an Italian name. For instance, Russ was really Sardie; Al was also Toto; Rose was called Sadie; Prudence was Provy; and Sal was called Tutti. I was really confused. Later when Sal and I had our children, Sal always gave each child a nickname. I guess it was a throwback to his family's ways.

I was impressed with Sal's father, Emanuele. I had not met anyone like him before. It is hard to find words to describe this colorful and unforgettable man. He gave the impression of being very tall, which he wasn't. He was of medium height. His martial posture, gained from serving in the Calvary of the Italian army, and his proud carriage combined to give him a very regal look. He had a full head of wavy black hair, twinkling, dark eyes and a well-groomed, handlebar moustache.

My first introduction to him left me in awe, but soon his earthy good humor put me at ease. He even asked me to dance and led me through the traditional dance, "The Tarantella." He had a strong Italian accent, but this only enhanced his charisma. He let me know he was the king in his family. In his broken English he told me, "I go nobody's house, everybody comma my house."

Since Sal and I only had a furnished room, this was not a problem.

Something clicked between my father-in-law and me at that first meeting and we had a wonderful rapport which was to last his lifetime. He was a very special man and I'm sorry he died before most of my children got to know their paternal grandfather. I will never forget him. Like the lyrics of a long-ago song say, "The memory lingers on."

Sal's mother was a little lady, always in an apron and always cooking for her large, extended family. She was a wonderful cook and meticulous housekeeper. I learned a great deal from her about cooking. Thanks to her, this Jewish girl learned how to make a delicious, Italian tomato sauce, great lasagna and other marvelous pasta dishes. My specialty is Italian/Jewish Chicken soup. It contains both pasta and matzo balls!

Mom Giglio didn't have much in the way of material possessions, but she kept her home the way she kept herself, always very neat and clean. In the little spare time she had, she did exquisite crocheting. She spoke only a little English and I knew no Italian, yet over the years I learned enough Italian to understand her and even speak a little Sicilian, which was the dialect the family used.

By the time we had been married twenty-five years and had several children, Sal's mother began to accept me and realize I was here to stay. A few years later, after Pop Giglio died, she came to live with us for awhile and we got along pretty well. We were even able to have short conversations. I learned some Yiddish when I was a child, so I guess I was multi-lingual. However, when I spoke with my mother-in-law and searched my mind for the Italian word I wanted to use, I often thought of the Yiddish word instead. This made my early attempts to converse in Italian very confusing.

After our short honeymoon over Arty's Windmill, our first home was in Brooklyn, New York. It was a furnished room with a smelly bathroom in the hall that we shared with four other people. It was owned by Mrs. Casa, otherwise known as, "the secret police landlady." She felt it was her right to unlock the door of our room and enter whenever she pleased. Often, we would return from an outing and find our things disturbed. Sometimes she would knock on the door once and if we happened to be in bed and didn't immediately answer, she would come in. This made for some very embarrassing moments. After all, we were newlyweds.

When the summer heat arrived, our one small room became unbearably hot and we had no ventilation. When we found out I was pregnant, we didn't know what to do. How could we raise a child in this furnished room? It seemed that having an abortion was the best solution. But, in 1947, abortion was illegal. Sal's brother-in-law had some ties to the underworld and he located a doctor for us who would do an illicit abortion. We went to see him. He examined me and we set a date for the procedure.

CHAPTER XIII

Baby Makes Three

As soon as I got off the examining table, for the first and only time in my life, I fainted dead away. Sal said the doctor panicked and said, "Forget about it. I wouldn't touch her with a ten foot pole."

Praise the Lord! We were so naïve, but for the Lord's intervention, I would have done something I would have had sorrow for the rest of my life.

The Orensteins, my mother's parents, asked us to move to Orlando, Florida, with them, and that was our plan. They did however make one stipulation. They asked my husband to change his name from Sal Giglio to Sol Gold. They didn't want anyone in Florida to know I had married a Gentile. Sal, much to my surprise, agreed to do that. While we were waiting for my grandfather to sell his property in Hempstead, New York, so we could move to Florida, he suffered a fatal heart attack, which put an abrupt end to our move south.

Well, we were not moving to Florida and we couldn't stay in the furnished room. So, we needed to make some decisions about our future because it wasn't just the two of us now. We had to think of our baby who would arrive in five months.

My dad invited us to come back home to the farm in Hightstown. We lived with my family for a month and then we rented a summer bungalow. Sal continued to work in the pizza restaurant while also working for my dad.

I finally had a chance to don an apron and try my hand at cooking. I followed cookbook directions exactly, yet my results rarely looked like the pictures in the books. Later, I was relieved to learn that the pictures in recipe books were often altered and retouched. Desserts were my specialty. This was before boxed mixes were available. Sal and I loved especially to bake marble cake. He was very good at swirling the chocolate batter through the yellow batter and I was superb in the icing department.

My pregnancy gave me one insatiable food craving—Jell-O. I just couldn't get enough, be it plain, fruited, or made into a salad. I would prepare the usual four servings for our dinner and consume them before lunch. I would then prepare another four servings and eat two of them before dinner.

In 1947, the year we moved back to Hightstown, my dad embarked on a new phase of farming. He was not only going to grow, slaughter, and market chickens, but he was also going to package chickens, cut up and ready to be cooked. He knew Sal was a tireless worker and asked him to partner with him in this new venture. Sal accepted, but he still kept his night job on Long Island.

He worked at the pizza restaurant on Long Island in New York four nights a week. The one-hundred-and-fifty mile round trip must have been exhausting for him, but he never complained. God has given Sal extraordinary energy. Even to this day, he can outwork much younger men.

The new operation on the farm was one of the first of its kind in 1947. This was before Frank Purdue and other chicken mavens got started. My father and Sal, my brothers Stan and Mel, and I worked tirelessly as a team in preparing the chickens for market. Before a new facility was built we worked outdoors, killing and plucking the feathers from the chickens.

Sal's father was a mason by trade and he undertook the building of the new facility that was needed. We were honored that my father-in-law, "the king," who never went to his children's homes, came to Hightstown and lived with us. He stayed about three months until the building was completed.

He and my dad developed a great love and respect for each other during this time. In the evening after work they would drink wine, sing together and trade stories. They had both been in the military and discovered they had much in common.

The cold December night before my first child was born I was working outside. My job was to swirl the freshly killed chickens in a vat of water that was kept hot over an open fire. This loosened the feathers so I could easily remove them. Talk about pioneer spirit! Later on, we had machines with rubber fingers that would remove the feathers.

While working that evening, I felt cramping in my stomach that grew steadily worse, though I didn't stop. I didn't realize until two a.m. when my water broke, that what I had been feeling were labor pains. I was about to become a mother!

Chapter XIV

A New Generation

t had snowed considerably during the night and our old car would not start. Sal roused one of the farm workers and borrowed his car for the fifteen-mile trip to the hospital. Slipping and sliding all the way, we made it safely to Princeton Hospital. Frances Carol was born on the morning of December 17, 1947.

With awe and wonder I gazed on this beautiful dark-haired little girl, my very own child. Though I was young, as I put her to my breast I felt every bit a mother. I thought of my own mother, sixteen years before, and wondered how she felt when she first saw me.

I had a wonderful sense that I was being used of God to start another generation. As was the custom in Italian families, we named our baby Frances after Sal's mother. We gave her the middle name Carol, which we called her, because she was born so near to Christmas. She was our Christmas Carol, the wonderful gift from God that we almost refused.

I felt very happy and I was determined to be a perfect mother. I wanted my daughter to have the happy childhood I had not had. Dr. Benjamin Spock's baby and childcare book was my constant reference. I did everything by the book. I didn't want advice from anyone.

I was still rebelling against adults telling me what to do. To say I was possessive of Carol and my role as her mother is an understatement. I felt that Dr. Spock and I could handle any problem that came along.

Carol's birth brought healing to my relationship with my step-mother. She was so happy to be a grandmother. She was skilled at knitting and she was constantly making adorable outfits for Carol. My brothers and sister loved being called uncle and auntie. Carol had a sweet disposition and a smile that melted everyone's heart.

From her earliest attempts, little Carol loved to help me in whatever I was doing. As her siblings were born, she became like a little mother to them. In fact, when the children were older, one of their friends asked, "How come your house has two mothers?" She will always be our Christmas Carol.

CHAPTER XV

Homeowners!

*I*n 1949 Sal sold chickens along with fresh eggs and vegetables. He established routes in nearby towns. In his travels he noticed one of the many post-World War II tracts of new homes in Edison, New Jersey. He told me about them and we visited the beautiful model home.

That day a strong desire to have his own home was birthed in my husband. We didn't have the money needed for a downpayment, so Sal started to work tirelessly toward that goal. Before long we had saved enough for the down payment.

We applied for—and got—a GI mortgage. This was a low interest loan that the government provided to ex-servicemen. That same year, 1949, we moved into 33 Morgan Drive, Edison, New Jersey. We were so proud to be Mr. and Mrs. Salvatore Giglio, Home Owners! We felt very mature and important.

What fun it was to decorate and furnish our own little nest. Our brand new home had two bedrooms, a kitchen, a living room and one bath. We also had an unfinished attic and a basement. It was small, but it was ours. We loved it.

We furnished our kitchen with a shiny chrome and Formica kitchen set. The tabletop was light gray adorned with two large red apples. Sal made a pattern of those apples and painted red apples on our white kitchen walls. They looked great. The rest of our home was furnished eclectically. Some furniture was given to us and we bought the rest. We still have a rocker that we proudly purchased in 1950.

Our lives took on new meaning. We joined the burgeoning group of WW II veterans who were becoming first-time homebuyers. Our mortgage was $9,500 and our monthly payments $60. My dad was worried that we would not be able to make the payments, but Sal assured him he would work as hard as was necessary to meet his new obligations.

Sal and I both took our responsibility as parents and spouses seriously. But, Sal was a lot more emotionally mature than I was. I had many unresolved needs in my life and I unrealistically expected him to meet them all. Getting married and escaping from my home solved some of my immediate problems, but I really didn't know how to cope with disappointments and offenses in a mature manner. When I couldn't have my way, I cried and had temper tantrums. It took a lot of patience on Sal's part to put up with my childlike behavior.

To my credit, I did recognize the need to change. I have always been an avid reader and I devoured self-help books. Be it the subject self-improvement, childcare, or marriage, I read and tried to put the things I learned into practice. Over the years, my desire to change and the process of maturing brought about significant growth in my life. But those early years were challenging for Sal.

We lived in a wonderful neighborhood where there was genuine camaraderie. Almost all of us had young children. We would baby-sit for each other, trade baby clothes, and recipes. We were all available for each other and ready to help be it illness, a new baby, or whatever.

No one had much money for evenings out, so we got together for parties several times a year. This was the early '50s, and life seemed so simple and innocent. There was a post-war spirit of hope and optimism. Stay-at-home moms were the norm. Dads were the sole breadwinners.

Society, schools and parents at that point in time, agreed on what was right and what was wrong. Kids still prayed in school and there was a respect for moral values. Children were taught to respect and defer to elders. Courtesy was taught in the schools and stressed by the parents. Virtuous living was much admired. Abortion was against the law. Divorce was considered a tragedy and viewed only as a last resort. Of course, people sinned as they always have and always will, but it was called sin, not choice or an alternative lifestyle.

As I look back, I see the forties as a time of great dependence on God when we, as a nation at war, prayed for peace in the world. We recoiled in disbelief at the horrific example of man's inhumanity to man in the Holocaust. The cataclysmic effect of the atom bomb was a grim reminder that war is hell.

The fifties were years of peace. It seemed God had answered our prayers and life returned to normal. We acknowledged God's care for us and we thanked Him. Our gratitude to Him was most evident in greater church attendance, and a building boom for churches of all denominations.

Though not all of us fully believed in God, we wanted our kids to believe. We had no idea that the ensuing decades would usher in the abolition of prayer in our public schools and a philosophy that would consider the existence of God an anachronism, and belief in Him superfluous.

49

Chapter XVI

We Got Religion
(but we didn't get it)

al's family was Roman Catholic. I was raised in a Jewish home. During our marriage, we never discussed religion. If asked, we would both say we believed in God, but Sal didn't go to church and I didn't go to synagogue. On Jewish holidays we celebrated with my family. Easter and Christmas were celebrated with Sal's family.

We decided we would not force either religion on our child. We would let her choose a religion when she was ready. We thought we were being very sophisticated and progressive. No mandatory religion for our family!

God, however, had other ideas. When I was nineteen I awakened one night in excruciating pain. Sal rushed me to the Doctor Farmer's Hospital in Allentown, New Jersey. I underwent an emergency operation. My appendix had burst and I was in critical condition. While I was under anesthesia and close to death, I seemed to hear God talk. I had never experienced any of this before, but somehow I knew it was He!

Basically, the message was "You say you believe in Me, but your life doesn't show it. You are sitting on a fence. You are luke-warm and I will spew you from my mouth."

I had never read the New Testament, so these words from Revelation 3:16 were new to me. Then I had what seemed to be a vision. I was shown a glimpse of what eternity would be like if God should "spew" me from His mouth. It was the most frightening sensation I have ever experienced. It seemed that I would whirl around in a gray void forever. I sensed a terrible feeling of aloneness and was shaken to the core of my being.

God revealed to me that we all will die someday and that determining our eternal destiny is the central purpose of human existence. We are given a choice. We can serve Him in this life and spend our eternity with Him in heaven or ignore Him, and spend eternity without Him.

After this experience, which stayed with me night and day, without a doubt or hesitation, I wanted to serve Him. I could not erase the memory or anxiety caused by what I had experienced while under anesthesia. It seemed my life hung in the balance and I had to make a choice.

I told Sal what I had experienced and urged him to talk with a priest to find out about going to church. I had decided that if he refused to do so, I would contact a rabbi. It didn't matter to me if it was a church or synagogue, I was determined our family would make God part of our lives and we had no time to lose.

Sal went to see Father Campbell, the Assistant Pastor at St. Paul's, the local Catholic Church, and told him of our situation. He invited Sal to come back with me. We went to see him the following week.

On that visit, Father Campbell explained to us the requirements for me to join the church. Since we had been married by a justice of the peace, the church didn't recognize ours as a valid marriage, so the first order of business was for us to be remarried in the church, in the sight of man and God. We asked our next door neighbors, the McGinns, to be witnesses to our marriage in a private church ceremony.

With that accomplished, the next order of business was for our daughter, Carol, who was now three years old, to be baptized. The Catholic Church teaches that without baptism the soul is condemned to hell. So, we lost no time in getting our child baptized.

The next step was for me to take a series of instructional sessions that would explain the doctrinal teaching of the Catholic Church. I was eager to plunge in and complete whatever process was necessary so I, too, could be baptized—saved from damnation. Much of what I learned was foreign to me, but Father Campbell told me to accept by faith what I could not understand. I felt like I was on a precarious bridge that led to God.

It was a wonderful day for me when I fulfilled all of the requirements of the catechism and I was baptized. Now, I felt safe! The very next Sunday we started attending Mass as a family. I felt a wonderful sense of belonging though I didn't understand everything. I knew God was my heavenly Father but I wasn't sure of what role Jesus and the Holy Ghost played. I recited their names by rote: Father, Son and Holy Ghost. But, I really didn't know who they were. I just wanted to serve God.

I tried to keep my conversion to Catholicism a secret from my Jewish family, but it was impossible. As our family grew there were many baptisms, first Holy Communions, Confirmations, and so on. My family never outwardly approved of my being a Catholic, but I think they resigned themselves to the thought that I became a Catholic for my husband's sake. The truth was my search for God brought Sal back to his religious roots.

For the next twenty-five years I lived an exemplary Catholic life, keeping the law down to the smallest detail. I really thought that this was what serving God was all about. I was determined to be the best Catholic ever! I had had a preview of what the after-life would be like without God and I did not want to take any chances with my eternal destiny. Ever since I was a little girl I believed God kept a book in which he wrote our good deeds and our bad. If there were more good deeds than bad when you died, you would go to heaven. When I became a Catholic, I took the Jewish God of my childhood and made Him a Catholic God. I thought becoming a Christian was a major good deed and I would be rewarded.

Our family's life revolved around our church. We attended services regularly and participated fully in the spiritual and social life of the church. There were holy days, novenas, dinners, dances, picnics and more. If it had to do with church, we were there.There were even parish talent shows in which Sal often starred. He joined the choir and his wonderful voice was soon put to use by the director. The choir sang beautiful Gregorian chants in Latin. Sal loved the sacredness of the Latin chant. He loved the honor of serving God with his voice.

In 1960 the Catholic Church began to use the vernacular, the language of the people, instead of Latin. Several years later when Sal stopped attending church he said one reason he left was that he did not like church music when it was sung in English. He felt it was not reverent enough. He had enjoyed being part of a choir that sang Gregorian chants. On the other hand, our kids really liked the new style, especially the folk masses.

CHAPTER XVII

Christmas at Last!

Now that I was Catholic, I was finally going to be able to celebrate Christmas in my own home. I was so excited I could not wait to make all of the things I had dreamed of as a child become real.

Sal shared my enthusiasm. He bought a beautiful crèche that was handmade in Italy. We still have it. Over time, the figurines started to break down. Each year before Christmas we would take our crèche from the attic only to discover some parts of the figurines had literally disappeared. Our youngest son Raphael (whom we'll meet later on) made up a ditty to the tune of "The Little Drummer Boy." It goes something like this,

> *See the manger per-um-pa-pum-pum*
> *There's just one king this year, per-um-pa-pum-pum*
> *The camel has one ear, par-um-pa-pum-pum*
> *The shepherds are not here, par-um-pap-um-pum.*

This is a typical display of our family's sense of humor. The one figurine that has remained unscathed by time is the baby Jesus.

Could that be because He is the same yesterday, today and tomorrow? It was more than likely a coincidence, but the truth still holds.

Sal decorated our home with many strings of outdoor Christmas lights, making our house the best decorated in the neighborhood. We bought our first Christmas tree and trimmed it with tinsel and other decorations. Of course, on the top we hung a beautiful angel with gossamer wings. I baked cookies, bought presents for everyone and, best of all; we went to church on Christmas Eve.

As time went on and our family increased, I tried to make each Christmas the best ever for each of the children. After awhile, Christmas shopping became a nightmare. I would shop 'til I dropped. I was obsessed with Christmas buying. I don't know if there is such a thing as a Christmas demon. But, if there is one, I had it!

It seemed I couldn't do enough, buy enough or prepare enough to make Christmas as wonderful for the family as I wanted it to be. I kept thinking of the "fantasy Christmas" in my mind as a child in New York. But, the joy of Christmas eluded me.

I didn't know what was missing. One thing for sure, it wasn't because of a lack of effort on my part. If it was camouflaged jackets that could only be found in an Army/Navy store miles away, I drove there. If it were a doll that not only cried, but also laughed fiendishly, I'd buy it. No effort was too great. If it were out there I would get it; no matter how many forays on cold wintry nights it took. I took each kid's wish list and tried to make all his or her wishes come true. Of course, I never succeeded. It was not that my kids were demanding, for they were not. They were grateful when they received new socks or underwear.

I was the problem! I was trying to give my kids the kind of Christmas I fantasized about when I was that little Jewish child. I had no history of how Christmas should be celebrated. I acknowledged that Christmas was the celebration of the Christ Child born to the Virgin Mary in a stable in Bethlehem, yet I missed the significance of Jesus.

I thought if I exhausted all my reserves of cash and energy, I was pleasing God by celebrating His Son's birthday. Despite my warped perception of the true celebration of Christmas, we had wonderful family times and I have many treasured memories.

As the family grew older we began to feel a need to do things for others, less fortunate then we. One year we adopted an entire family and we bought them clothing, toys and food. Another year the family brought a home-cooked Christmas dinner with turkey and all the trimmings to a homeless shelter. Some of us filled shoeboxes for operation Christmas Child. These gift-filled boxes were distributed to needy children all over the world.

I have always felt it is important to set an example of loving others instead of just talking about it.

CHAPTER XVIII

Cheaper by the Dozen

We quickly learned that the Catholic Church didn't allow the practice of birth control. Only the rhythm method of natural family planning was sanctioned. Because I could not carry a tune I joked that the "rhythm method" would never work for me. Sure enough, we ended up with a family of twelve, six sons and six daughters. I truly believe this was God's will for my life. As far as I am concerned, He planned for each child to be born.

Blond, smiling Diane joined our family in June of 1951. Carol, who was three, loved her baby sister. She was always ready to amuse her and help me in caring for her. While Carol was on the shy side, Diane was outgoing.

From the day she was born, Diane had a very happy disposition, smiling and cooing all the time. We called her our "Sunshine girl." All through her school years, our home was filled with her friends. It seemed people were naturally attracted to her. She was a good athlete and a great basketball player. Her love for people led her to become a nurse. She had a special compassion for the terminally ill. Diane was popular and had many boyfriends. But, when she met this special person at the church she was attending she felt he was the man God wanted her to marry. Their marriage seemed good at first, but then dark clouds appeared on the horizon.

Her husband became very controlling. She could not go anywhere, do anything or even wear anything without his express permission. We worried about her, but she never complained or vented her misgivings about her marriage. We were reluctant to interfere, so our reaction was limited to prayer.

They had three children very close in age, Jacob, Lucas and Sunday. Soon after the last baby was born, Diane became depressed and tried to take her life. She came home to stay with us. Eventually her severe depression required hospitalization on several occasions.

In the meantime, her husband divorced her and took custody of their children. All of her anger, hostility and blame were directed to me. The things she would say to me and about me hurt terribly. It was an extremely painful time.

Yet it brought me to a stronger dependence on God. Many times I prostrated myself before God and asked Him to search me and reveal anything that I had done to cause Diane's illness. After much prayer, I felt vindicated by God, realizing that Diane could believe things to be true when they were not.

Life is not easy for Diane. She still struggles with mental illness. It is so hard, both for the one who is ill and those who love her. There have been rays of hope. Those moments encourage us to believe that someday she will be healed and her sunny, happy self will re-emerge.

Chapter XIX

The Three Boys

*I*n July of 1952, our first son was born. Sal was elated to have a son, after two daughters. He hung a huge banner across the front of our house that read, "It's A Boy!"

According to the Italian custom of naming the firstborn for the paternal grandfather, we named him Emanuel. Since there were already two boys called Emanuel in the family, we called our son by his middle name, Richard.

He was born post-mature, three weeks after my due date. He weighed nine pounds and was twenty-four inches long. He was a pitiful sight, just skin and bones. Richard did not receive enough nourishment to sustain him during the extra three weeks he spent in my womb. After his first week home, he became very ill and had to go back to the hospital. We spent every spare moment visiting him. It was a very anxious time for us.

He showed little improvement. The pediatrician decided to send him to a New York City hospital for further diagnosis. But, he suggested our taking him home for a week between hospitalizations. Richard could not tolerate milk, so we fed him a high protein substitute. Each time he'd cry we would feed him and within three days he started to gain weight. This was an answer to many prayers and an example of God's ongoing mercy to our family, for he recovered without further hospitalization.

God has used our first-born son to lead many people to Himself. He served for a few years in Youth With A Mission (YWAM) then spent time in Israel and worked on a kibbutz. As is often the case with an oldest son, Rich and his dad had some strong disagreements. On one of his visits home he was convinced that he needed to honor his dad.

The way he chose to make peace was to wash his father's feet. Sal didn't want any part of that ritual. The scene that ensued was hilarious. Rich ran after his dad with a towel and basin of water, up the stairs and down the stairs. Sal finally yelled, "Do it to your mother. She likes that Christian stuff, I don't!"

From the time Rich was a child he loved to sing. He later went on to play many instruments well. Diane and he were thirteen months apart, and by the time they were two and three, they looked like twins. They loved to sing for us and would put on little shows.

When they got older, they called themselves, "Dick and Dee Dee." They would turn their school blazers inside out and wear them with the shiny green lining on the outside and sing duets. This was the beginning of a lot of homegrown entertainment, for many of our children are musically gifted and they didn't hesitate to show it.

In my home when I was growing up no one could carry a tune. This was unbelievable to Sal, because everyone in his family could sing well. He thought everyone could at least sing on key. But this was not so with my father's family. I learned early on what I was. When I was in third grade, the music teacher listened to each one in the class sing a scale. When she cocked her ear next to me, she proclaimed, "You are a listener."

I guess these days I would be called, "musically challenged."

Sal passed his gift and love for music on to most of the children. We have always had music in our home. Some of our children have also married gifted musicians.

Thomas joined our family in June of 1954. Now we had what Sal believed was the ideal family. Each girl had a sister and each boy had a brother. What more could anyone ask for?

Tommy was what was known as a jumpy baby. We had to be oh-so-gentle when we picked him up and laid him down so he would not be frightened. The other children loved it when Sal rough housed with them, but not our Tom. He had an invisible sign that said, "Handle with Care."

Yet, Tom grew up to be the most athletic and outspoken of all our children.

Long Beach Island was his favorite surfing spot along the Jersey shore. Each summer as a teenager he would spend as much time as he could there.

He left college in his second year to buy a business, which was the first of several successful ventures. He has worked with two of his brothers and now with his own sons. Tom went back to college when his fifth son was born and earned a Masters of Social Work degree.

It appeared we were in the baby business. My menstrual cycle was very irregular and that is not compatible with use of the "rhythm method."

Peter was born in 1955. He was a beautiful chubby baby and looked like a big rubber doll. While Tommy was a jumpy baby, Peter was a very placid baby. He loved watching his older brothers' wrestle and play and before we knew it, he was joining them.

All three boys were blond and very cute. When I look back at the pictures of my children as youngsters, feelings of love, nostalgia, and a sense of sadness come over me. I am amazed at what beautiful children they were. I wonder, "Where was I and why can't I remember those days?"

I think because I was so busy caring for them, I just didn't take the time to ever step back and look at them.

Peter, Tommy and Rich formed the group we referred to as "The Three Boys." They were so close in age they did everything together. They worked together, played together and, sadly, got into drugs together.

Peter is a man of quiet strength, but his love and devotion to Jesus speaks volumes to me.

He was still living at home when he asked Jesus to be his Savior. It was the remarkable change I saw in him that helped draw me to the Savior. I would often wake up early to care for the baby of the household and I would find Peter on his knees or reading his Bible. He would patiently explain the Gospel to me, though I wasn't yet ready to receive it. When he married his wife, Shirley, I asked him what he loved most about her, he replied, "I haven't met another girl who loves Jesus as much as she does."

Peter and Shirley and their children live in Maryland. He is active in his church and following in his dad's footsteps, he owns a large garage door business.

Chapter XX

Enlarging our Tents

We seemed to be busting out all over. We had outgrown our family sedan and we bought our first in a series of nine passenger station wagons. Now no one had to sit on the floor or lie across the ledge under the back window as they had been doing in order to all fit in our car. When we stopped for traffic lights the other drivers would do a double take when they saw the many little passengers peering out the many windows. I often thought I should put a sign in the window that said, "Yes, they are all mine!"

It was no easy task to keep the children from fussing especially on long trips. I invented and re-invented license plate and count the colored cars games. The reward would be an M&M for each out of state license or red car. I got a lot of mileage out of a twelve-ounce bag of M&Ms.

When they were older and misbehaved while I was driving I would issue two warnings to settle down—or else. If they didn't obey my warning I would swing my big black shoulder bag back, holding on to the strap like a bolo. They got very good at ducking out of its path.

Our little house also seemed to be growing smaller as our family grew larger. Even though we had two sets of bunk beds in each bedroom and Sal and I slept in the partially finished attic, we were decidedly overcrowded. It was time to look for a larger home. We all piled into our Ford station wagon and set off to find a new home.

We had paid $9,500 when we bought our original house. We sold it for $12,000 six years later. The profit allowed us to put a downpayment on a much larger new home in North Brunswick, New Jersey. We moved into our new home in June 1956, with our five children and another baby on the way!

Our new home seemed so spacious. It was a split-level. It had seven and one-half rooms. The two baths were especially welcome! When Sal picked out a lot for it, he chose one next to a proposed playground. What a boon that proved to be!

When school ended in the spring, the summer playground program began. A few days before the official program kicked off, the herald of a good summer arrived. A large truck delivered a huge green box of playground equipment and games. Because they lived next to the park, my kids were the first to know. They would ride around our development on their bikes announcing, "The Green Box is here!"

Living next to the park was very convenient. It was like having a summer camp in my backyard. It was safe to send the children out to play in the park. I could keep an eye on them through the window and ring the dinner bell for them to come home for meals. Besides living next to the playground, we were close to the woods and a lake. The posted signs around the water read, "Boating and Fishing Only—No Swimming."

I think my boys probably held the world record for accidentally falling into the lake. It happened quite often when they swung out on rope swings like Tarzan and, "whoops!" Our children had the good fortune to be raised in a wonderful location. Building a tree house, fishing, and "falling into" the lake kept them busy during the summer months. In the winter when the lake was frozen, they would go ice-skating. Each snowfall brought out a brigade of sleds. They could sled a quarter-mile from the end of our property to the lake edge.

We taught each one that they were placed in our particular family for a reason, and that it was a privilege to be part of a big family. With the privilege came responsibility, so each child was given a chore according to age and capability. Most chores were performed after school and Saturday mornings. This left Saturday afternoon free for fun times like trips to the zoo, beach or museums. Sundays were for church and family visiting.

It was God's grace that kept us from feeling overburdened by the responsibility of our large family. I have always thought God would not give us this family if He didn't know we could care for them. Sal worked more hours and my patience stretched a little further. We loved our life and we were proud of our family. We truly felt each child was a gift from God.

CHAPTER XXI

Rosemary, Plinky and Monica

osemary, our third daughter, was born in December of 1956, the same year we moved into our new—and present—home. She looked like a little princess. Rosie, as we called her, was a very good baby. Both Carol and Diane took turns mothering her, taking her for walks and reading to her. It seemed that what I wasn't able to give the children in the way of individual time and attention their older siblings supplied.

It was usual in those days to stay in the hospital for five days with each birth. After the first twenty-four hours of recuperation the rest of the time was like a mini-vacation. It was fun to spend time with the other new mothers oohing and cooing over our little ones. I wasn't like some new mothers anxious to get back home. I knew what was waiting for me at home so I took full advantage of my time in the hospital! There I had nothing to do, but nurse my baby and make myself look pretty for my visitors.

Rosie has been a wonderful daughter. It was her job to fold and distribute the three or more loads of wash I did each day. She helped in many other ways as well, but laundry was her main chore. This, she continued until she married at age twenty-five. She has remained close to her family and is always willing to help.

Rosie met her dream guy Glen when she was a senior in High School. It was love at first sight for each of them. She got a job as a secretary after she graduated, and Glen pursued a career as a musician. After a lengthy courtship, they married. Glen is now a well-known composer and musician. His career necessitates his traveling a great deal. When Rosie and the children are able, they travel with him. When they cannot, Rosie keeps the home fire burning brightly while Glen lights up the world with his music.

Salvatore Junior joined our growing family in 1959. I figured that after producing four sons, Sal deserved to have a son named for him.

Ten days after he came home from the hospital he started to experience projectile vomiting. Unless one has experienced this with a child, one can't imagine the force with which a seven pound baby can throw up food. It was absolutely terrifying.

The pediatrician, suspicious of what the cause was, sent us to a surgeon. After tests in the hospital, our baby was diagnosed with Pyloric Stenosis. This is a condition in which the pyloric valve closes up and the baby cannot retain food. The only remedy is surgery. Without it, the baby will starve to death.

It was very hard to sign the permission papers to allow the operation, but we knew we had no choice. It was heartbreaking to hand our baby over for a procedure we weren't sure he could survive. Sal and I spent the three hours during the operation in the hospital chapel pleading for our son's life. God once again showed us His favor. Although little Salvatore's recovery was slow and he didn't regain his birth weight until he was two months old, he overcame his fragile beginning and grew up healthy.

"Plinky," as we called him, was a bona fide child prodigy. At three years he began playing the piano. He would crawl onto the bench as soon as he awakened in the morning and play tunes he said he dreamed about in the night. By age six, he would lay on the floor in front of the stereo and listen for the piano parts in his older brothers' record albums. Then he would play them by ear. He always seemed to be "plinking" out a tune. His nickname, Plinky, even appears on music he now writes and produces.

Because he was obviously gifted we felt an obligation to help him develop his gift by giving him piano lessons. But, he stymied all our attempts and frustrated half-a-dozen teachers. He insisted on learning on his own—and he did. He would entertain us by playing any song anyone could hum. Today, he is a popular music arranger and producer.

He married Laura when he was twenty. I didn't think he was mature enough to marry. Look who's talking! I guess I was wrong. They have beautiful daughter.

Our feisty little Monica was born in 1961. We named her for Sister Monica who had held prayer vigils at the church beseeching God for Plinky to be healed. The first two weeks of her life were typical infant days. But when she was three weeks old, to our horror, she started displaying the same symptoms Plinky had when he was an infant. This time we didn't even stop at the pediatrician's office. We went straight to the surgeon. He confirmed our fears.

This wasn't supposed to happen. Pyloric Stenosis, again? This is not a genetic disease and did not run in families. Yet, at three weeks old, Monica had to undergo the same surgery her older brother had. Because Monica was two weeks older than Plinky when he had the surgery, she was stronger and her recuperation was quicker.

Come to think of it, Monica did everything quickly. She always was strong-minded, and when she set her sights on doing something, she did it fast and did it well. I remember one time we had a small fire in the house, and Monica called the Fire Department. She told them, "This is only a small fire; just send one truck." A few minutes later two fire trucks, an ambulance and a police car came racing down our street. Monica ran over to them and admonished them saying, "I distinctly ordered *one* fire engine." She was about ten at the time.

She finished high school in three years by taking heavy class loads. She then went on to graduate from nursing school. Unfortunately, her marriage ended in 1998 after nineteen years.

She is coping as a single mom. She has a busy life—juggling a career and three lively children. But Monica is a very capable person with fortitude, and she is doing an excellent job in balancing her work life and her mothering.

CHAPTER XXII

Eight Is Not Enough

e now had four girls and four boys. Eight children seemed like a good round number. Keeping our large family supplied with groceries was no easy task. It seemed I was always shopping. Sal said I should have had a bumper sticker that read, "I brake for supermarkets."

If it is "cheaper by the dozen," you couldn't prove it by our food bill. Sal always worked hard and our larder was never empty. His prayer to God was, "God, I will do the work and You do the worrying." This proved to be a good arrangement and our family always had what we needed.

Shopping was a huge project. Unfortunately, neither wholesale nor bulk buying was available when I needed them. I usually got a baby sitter to stay with the young ones while I made my foray to the supermarkets with a couple of the older kids.

We quickly filled two grocery carts. The kids had a special name for groceries. There was "food", which consisted of the basics like rice, potatoes, onions, pasta, and so on and then there was "fode", which consisted of cookies, snacks and other goodies. Cereal was a big item on our grocery list. And, because I allowed the older kids to

73

buy their favorite cereal, this fell into the "fode" classification unless, of course, it was oatmeal.

There was a two-year period when work was very scarce and so was money. For the first time, I signed up for food stamps—a government-funded program.

We had never needed public assistance and I was embarrassed to be using it. I would go to an agency two towns over to get the food stamps. Then I'd shop in a store where no one knew me. I was very glad when our business improved and I didn't need to use food stamps anymore. As I look back now, I see it as God's provision for us. Then, it was a source of shame to me. Now, I am thankful that programs exist for struggling families in hard times.

Getting our large family ready for church was a huge task, starting with baths and shampoos on Saturday nights. Before they were old enough to bathe themselves, baths became an assembly line job. I was the washing machine. I would soap and rinse them, then hand each child to Sal. He became the drying machine.

I would lay out their clothes the night before and invariably the girls would want to wear something different. Surprisingly, the boys liked to get dressed up. Sal always left early to get ready to sing in the choir. So, the responsibility for getting our act together fell on me. When I finally got them all piled into the station wagon, I was ready for a nap instead of Mass.

Our family filled a pew and earned a lot of admiring looks from those in the congregation whom enjoyed seeing large families. Some looks, however, seemed to say, "Better you than me!" Little did they—or we—suspect that our family would keep growing.

Chapter XXIII

Jigs and the Pigs

In 1963 our fifth son joined our family. We picked the name Joseph because of the two men in the Bible named Joseph whom God used so powerfully. We also had Joe Woods in mind, a very kind and gentle friend.

Our Joseph was a cute and energetic handful. He had a special talent for creating chaos. When his siblings would play a board game, he delighted in flipping the board and sending the game pieces flying. If he encountered a pile of freshly folded laundry, he felt obligated to push it over. It is a good thing he was so cute and lovable, or his brothers might have sold him to a passing caravan like Joseph's family did in the Book of Genesis.

Joe's teen years were tumultuous but God began to get through to him. When he was sixteen, he had a genuine salvation experience. He was a changed teenager. He told his friends in school about Jesus and led his girlfriend to the Lord.

He had a popular rock group called "Jigs and The Pigs." Drugs became the greedy monsters in his life and, except for the grace of God, they almost destroyed him. It seemed he had defeated the monsters when he rededicated his life to God and married for the first time. But drugs attacked again, even more savagely, and he lost his wife, his house and his marriage. He hit the bottom of the pit, but he was in a place God could reach him.

Joe knew he needed supernatural help. He spent three months in a Christian rehab program. As he reached out for Jesus, Jesus lifted him out of the miry pit and set him on a rock. His life was turned around and he received healing in many areas of his life. He rededicated his life to the Lord and God has used him and his music in powerful ways. Wherever Joe is, whether on the job or at the gym he senses the need for God in others and he shares Jesus with them.

When he came out of the rehabilitation program, he married Debbie, who had faithfully stood by him through all his ups and downs. Joe has a terrific son born during his first marriage and he and Debbie have an adorable daughter. Joe or "Jigs" as he prefers to be called, runs the family business, Bristol Garage Doors, which will someday be his. His story illustrates God's faithfulness.

CHAPTER XXIV

Angels Among Us

One evening in 1963 Sal and I took the bus to New York City to meet some friends and go to the theater. Normally we drove into the city, but this time we did it "the easy way." The bus parked in the huge Port Authority terminal. In our hurry we didn't notice the platform number where our bus was parked.

We had a wonderful evening and got back to the terminal with very little time to spare. We planned to take the last bus home except we didn't know which one to get on and there was no one around to ask. To say Sal and I were panicky is an understatement. We felt as though we were in a maze as we raced from one boarding platform to another.

With only two minutes left we raced up the escalator. Just as we reached the top, a handsome young man in blue jeans and a black leather jacket suddenly stepped out of the crowd and approached us. He pointed to the right and said, "The bus to New Brunswick is that way."

We hurriedly thanked him and got on just as it was about to leave. When we were seated, I asked Sal who the young man was.

He told me he didn't know him and that he assumed I did. I immediately said, "It must have been an angel!" My knowledge of angels, if I thought of them at all, was limited to little cherubs with wings. I had no idea they could assume human form. Yet, I was sure the young man who helped us was really an angel.

The next Sunday I told our priest about our encounter and he said, "Of course, that was Saint Raphael. He is sent to help people who are lost." He then went on to say, "The next son you have you must name him Raphael."

At that time we had nine children and another child was not on our agenda. Yet, fourteen months later I gave birth to a beautiful nine-pound baby boy. Guess what we named him?

Raphael was born October 21, 1964, within three days of the day Catholics celebrate the Feast of Saint Raphael. Was it coincidence or was it God's way of showing us He was involved in all areas of our lives?

Raphael invited Jesus to be Lord of his life when he was ten years old, as he says, "through the ministry of my Jewish Grandfather who was crazy about the Messiah." Almost immediately he started writing songs about the Lord. His music helped many teens come to salvation at the concerts Raphael played during high school.

On the recommendation of his close friend, Phil Keaggy, Raphael and his wife moved to Nashville, Tennessee in 1994. But a sudden and unexpected end to his marriage devastated Raphael. He sought healing by leaving Nashville and moving back to New Jersey. He enrolled in computer training courses. Soon he landed a great job in the computer field in New York City.

In 1997, a Nashville producer who was impressed with Raphael's music, convinced him to return to Nashville and record a CD for a new label he was starting. Raphael means, "God heals." His songs have, indeed, brought hope and healing to many people through his concerts and recorded music.

He is now a Co-Pastor of New River Fellowship Church in Nashville. He also travels periodically doing concerts and ministering the Word of God.

Ten children were plenty—as had been eight or six or "the perfect four." But, once again God saw fit to expand our family. I sincerely believe that each child born is by the direct will of God. It takes more than a mother and father; it also takes God to breathe life into each soul.

There were times when, discovering I was pregnant, I cried out, "God, I can't do this again!" But, His still, small voice would reassure me that by His grace, I could. I found great peace in believing that He knows my capabilities better than I do and He would not send a child I was unable to love and nurture. A mother's heart, I have found, is quite expandable.

Deborah was born two-and-one-half years after Raphael. She was a beautiful baby with delicate features. She was named after my dad's mother. I loved Bubeh, and I was glad I could honor her memory by giving one of my daughters her name. If you have enough children you get to give them all your favorite names and honor your favorite people.

Debbie was a sweet and docile little child. From the time she was a toddler she loved to sing. But, because she was shy, we really had to coax to get her to perform for us.

When she was thirteen she became a passionate Christian and led a number of her friends to the Lord. She was influenced by some over-zealous Christian friends to smash her worldly records. However, the pendulum eventually swung the other direction and as she grew older she rebelled against Christian values.

When she was eighteen she formed her own band that played her original music. Debbie or Brijitte, her stage name, has given me the opportunity to meet some interesting people. When she was living in New York I came into the City to spend the day with her. She asked me whether I would mind if a friend joined us for lunch. I told her that it would be fine with me.

That was the day Church Lady (me) lunched with a member of a very famous and raucous rock group. I actually was impressed with the good manners and courtesy shown me by this famous—or infamous—young man.

Debbie is so talented she sings like an angel. And, though she is still shy in family settings, when she plays her guitar and sings on stage, her many fans love her.

She is married to Peter, a drummer, and they have combined their musical talents to form a great band. Their band has traveled across the country and played in many venues as the opening act for famous rock stars. Though I may in principle disapprove of the type of music she was identified with, I've never disapproved of her and my love for her never wavered. As she has matured, so has her music. The songs she writes are absolutely beautiful.

In case you have been counting, after Debbie the score was six sons and five daughters. You know what that meant. We had to even out the numbers. So, along came Elena, our baby. I don't know why God blessed us with six sons and six daughters, but I am glad He did. Doesn't it sound so orderly?

By the time Elena was born most of her older brothers and sisters were teenagers. I can remember Rich, our oldest son, who was a high school senior at the time, bringing a bunch of his friends to the house to see the new baby. What a priceless picture to see these brawny guys oohing and cooing over a pink and white bassinet!

Elena had several older siblings anxious to parent her. One day at mealtime one of the older ones fed her a jar of baby food and then left. A few minutes later someone else came by, noticed it was dinnertime, and also fed her. She promptly threw up. After that, I made all the decisions about her feeding schedule.

She has a wonderful, happy disposition and loved all the attention she received from her siblings.

Elena and Debbie, two years apart in age, grew up together. Though they had many very heated disagreements, they were and still are as young wives, closely bonded to each other. Debbie was the quiet, shy one and Elena was the outgoing one.

As toddlers the two schemed together. Debbie would quietly come up with ideas and Elena would carry them out. For instance, after they were in bed for the night in their shared room, Debbie would tell Elena to go to the kitchen and get cookies out of the cookie jar. Elena would get caught in the act and be reprimanded. Debbie would say, "I'm a good girl, aren't I, Mommy?"

Elena is very artistic and thought art would be her chosen profession. That is, until a mean-spirited designer she worked for seemed to take pleasure in denigrating her work. He soon squashed her creativity and she left the profession. She switched careers, receiving training as a cosmetologist. Now, she is using her creative talents as a hair stylist at an upscale salon.

In 1997 she married the love of her life, Steve Mattey, in a picturesque ceremony on the beach. Several young nieces and nephews, all dressed in white, were members of the wedding party. It was like a storybook wedding.

The occasion also marked the first time in twelve years all our children were together. It was a wonderful time and a heartwarming family reunion.

CHAPTER XXV

Flying Kids and Flopping Fish

Through the years of child bearing and child rearing, God's grace was more than sufficient. He gave me strength to care for our family and He gave Sal the health and ability to support our family.

He also gave us wisdom in how to discipline our children. Even though each child had a different disposition, we had certain rules that were not negotiable. One was that they never strike each other. As girls sometimes will, they would provoke the boys. We assured the boys we would mete out the appropriate punishment for transgressions against them, and we did.

Our aim was that the children would grow up with a deep respect for others. We have seen the fruit of that in our children as they have grown into adults. I am very proud of the respect they show their wives, husbands and others.

Another rule was that the boys were not allowed to rough house with each other indoors. Our home was to be a house of peace, not a prize fighting or wrestling arena. The admonition, "Take it outside," curtailed many fisticuffs, especially during inclement weather.

Back when the kids were young, I would leave the house appointing the oldest teen to be in charge. One day I arrived home from grocery shopping to see the younger children flying out of the TV room. I looked in the room and there was Rich ready to launch another kid out. He was standing ankle deep in water and all our tropical fish were jumping around on the carpet!

Somehow, mysteriously, our huge fish tank had crashed to the floor dumping all its water and fish. Rich was trying to protect the kids from broken glass and trying to keep the fish from asphyxiation. What a mess! Rich managed to rescue most of the fish, but it took a week for the carpet to dry.

We tried to instill in our children the idea that God ordained our large family, and each of us to be a part of it. Because we believed that to be true, we believed it was each child's responsibility to be involved in whatever it took to maintain our household.

Each had a chore appropriate to his age and abilities. We found that if they worked in pairs, it made the job much easier. For instance a three-year-old and a five-year-old could carry a trash bag room to room and empty wastepaper baskets. A ten-year-old and a twelve-year-old could wash and dry dishes. Two teenage boys could do a bang-up job of mopping and waxing floors, especially if they were told, "No work, no play."

Children may not be cheaper by the dozen, but a dozen helpers made the housework much easier. Another benefit, as our friends often begrudgingly reminded us, we had built-in babysitters.

I was cautious not to burden the children with responsibilities that were not appropriate since, after all, they were children. I tried to insure that each one would have a happy and carefree childhood.

Besides nurturing, Sal and I tried to inculcate traditional values into their lives. We celebrated traditional, patriotic, and Christian holidays. As Catholics, we honored Mary the mother of Jesus by saying the rosary as a family devotion, and we always said grace before meals. I can remember saying to the younger children gathered around the table, "Don't eat that yet, it is hot; let's say grace." Somehow the idea was formed that saying grace cooled the food.

This worked, for occasionally one of the little ones would say, "Say grace again, it is still hot."

Family values such as respect for each other and the upholding of our family name was stressed in a lot of different ways. Because there were so many of us people watched us rather closely. I knew the misdeeds of even one of the children could reflect on the whole family. I helped them understand that each one was an ambassador representing our family, and it was important for them to conduct themselves in a way that reflected positively on our family.

Did they always do that? No, of course not. But for the most part they tried, and our family was highly thought of. People often commented that our children were very respectful and well mannered. When we had company in the evenings, our guests would comment on how quiet our house was.

Bedtime was not an option in our house. The younger kids were put to bed by seven and by seven-thirty the last bedtime story was read and the last drink of water was given. The older children were given an extra half-hour according to their age. Nevertheless, by nine o'clock all twelve would be in their rooms sleeping, reading or studying. I don't think this traumatized any of them. Besides, Sal and I needed some quiet time after our extremely full and busy days.

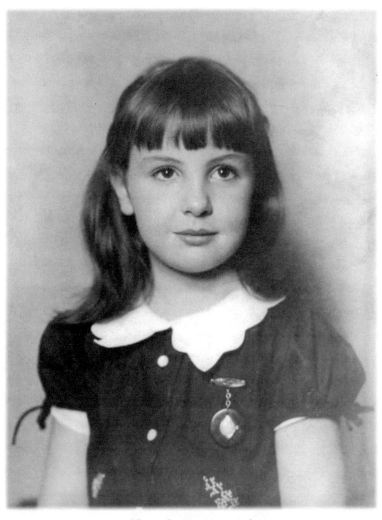

Here I am at age 9
The age in which I began to know that
God had more for me!

Tomberg Family Wedding
Mother is first from the left with Dad behind her.

Sal's parents, brothers and sisters
— large Italian family—in 1947.

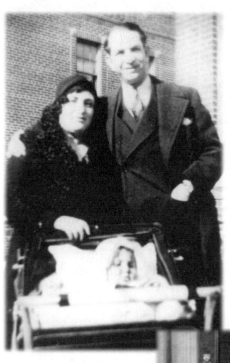

*The only photo
I have of my
parents with me.
My mother had
no idea she would
not live to see my
first birthday!*

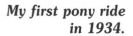

*My first pony ride
in 1934.*

My brother Stan and I in 1940.
Stan has always made me smile!

At 17, I'm a wife and mother!

My handsome husband, Sal Giglio,
in 1945 during WWII.

Sal and I in 1947.

Sal and I celebrating 50 years 1997.

Family portraits were always an adventure!
Here are Carol, Diane, Rich, Tom, Peter,
Rosemary, Sal Jr. "Plink" and Monica.

What a crew! A rare photo of all 12 children.
From left to right: Carol, Diane, Rich, Tom,
Peter, Rosemary, Sal Jr. "Plink" Monica,
Joe, Raphael, Debbie and Elena.

Graduation Day!
May, 1999
I made it—by God's Grace!

CHAPTER XXVI

Short Summer Days and the Long Winter

he seashore, to me, is the closest thing to heaven on this earth. My children share this love. We took lots of day trips to the beach. I would schlep the station wagon with playpen, coolers, beach umbrella, beach toys, towels, any other number of necessary items, and at least six children. Then, we would unload and we would again schlep everything onto the beach.

Whenever we could afford it the children and I would spend a week during the summer at the shore. One late spring I went to the Jersey shore to see about a place we could rent for a week that summer, stopping at the location of a beach cottage where we met the owner. "It is perfect," I said. "My kids will love it!"

"How many children do you have?" he asked.

I didn't want to scare the poor man with the vision of twelve children romping through his property. The truth was half of the kids had jobs and wouldn't be with us. I was caught on the horns of a dilemma. I didn't want to lie, but I was afraid if I said "twelve" he would not rent to us. So, I quickly tried to remember how many kids I had brought with me, still waiting in the car.

"Four or five," I cautiously answered. He looked at me rather suspiciously, but rented to us anyhow.

One of the added benefits of our vacations was that we were more or less corralled together. We did crafts on rainy days, flew kites, collected shells and just spent time together. Without the distractions of telephones, playmates, baseball games and so on, I got the opportunity to reconnect with my kids during these summer hiatuses. Sal never vacationed with us. Have you ever seen a man with long pants, black shoes, and socks on the beach? That would be Sal. He found no joy in the sand and surf.

It was common in those days for the husband to be the sole wage earner, and for the wife to stay at home with the children. Fortunately, God supplied Sal and me with tremendous energy and endurance. He worked sixty hours a week and I am sure I matched that as I worked in the home taking care of our family.

Unfortunately, we didn't take such good care of our relationship. The demands of a large family easily obscured serious problems in our marriage. Looked at from the outside, we appeared to be a big happy family. But things were not as they seemed. Early in the seventies, during the "do your own thing" era, our marriage came apart.

My son Raphael had written a song telling about a little boy who would put things on the railroad track so they would be flattened when the train wheels ran over them. He kept all of his flattened treasures in a box. The boy could always feel the rumble and hear the whistle of the oncoming train. He always got out of the way in time.

One fateful day the old diesel was replaced by the new DSX, which hardly made a rumble, and didn't make a sound. They found the box of flattened things, but that was all they found.

This song has been interpreted in many ways even though it talks about a little boy and trains. Perhaps the most apt construction is that we go along in life thinking we know what to watch out for until, suddenly, everything changes. You never see it coming.

That's what happened to me. I thought my life was together and I was in control of the events in my family's life. I thought I had all my treasures in a box.

One day Sal said, "I am going to live my life my way. You have been choosing our friends, directing our social life; now I am going to do what I want to do."

I was taken by complete surprise. I never saw it coming. I thought Sal was as satisfied with our life as I was.

Sal had acquired some younger friends who had a lifestyle very different from that of our church and family. He started going out to lunch and didn't come home for dinner. He often didn't return until it was almost morning. It seemed we had been walking down a path together and now he was taking a side road without me. Soon, he lost interest in me.

How could this be happening? Wasn't I the perfect Catholic, the perfect wife, the perfect mother, the perfect everything? I didn't know what to do. As the days turned into weeks I became panicky and frantic. After bearing and nurturing twelve beautiful children for my husband, I felt like I was a failure. The pain of feeling that I had failed as a wife and was losing Sal was incredible. My heart was shattered. I had no control over this maelstrom that was destroying us. I was coming apart and I didn't know where to turn for help.

Then I did something I never thought I would do. Like my dad before me, I turned to alcohol. I had suffered as a child because of my dad's drinking and now I began to create the same environment for my kids. The guilt and shame I felt was terrible, yet the alcohol took the edge off my pain. I kept a quart of vodka hidden in the laundry hamper. It became my anesthesia.

My family was completely ignorant of my problem. Pride and shame kept me from exposing the cancer that was destroying us as a family. I had been taught that what goes on behind closed doors should stay there. We never talked about what went on in the house. Before long, I could barely function. I felt as though I were about to fall into a deep dark pit. I clung to the edge of sanity just by my fingertips. Then I felt my fingers start to slip.

CHAPTER XXVII

Out of Egypt

I knew I needed help. I finally began to see a psychiatrist who put me on medication. I also started to see a therapist. After six weeks of sessions, my therapist asked me how I would feel if she didn't see me anymore.

When she asked that question I had an epiphany. It was as though the heavens opened and a huge banner came down bearing in large letters, the word, ABANDONED. A tremendous change swept into my life. I began to realize how much the fear of abandonment caused by my mother's death and the guilt of thinking it was my fault, persisted in coloring and controlling my life. Now, I felt powerless as my husband also abandoned me.

As I learned more about myself, I realized things I had never thought of before. It was as though God gave me a revelation. I began to feel I was a person of worth. It was absolutely liberating to understand that my worth was not contingent on Sal's feelings toward me. I would not have been surprised to see my picture as the poster child for co-dependency!

I decided I would learn to be independent. I borrowed a line from an old song, "I got along without you before I met you and I'll get along without you now." It became my anthem. This was the early 1970s and the Feminist Movement was in full swing. While I could not completely embrace the creed of the Women's Movement, I was empowered by some of their philosophy. However, I wasn't about to burn my bra until the Women's Liberation leaders could do away with gravity's effect on my bosom after nursing twelve children!

I was angry at Sal for emotionally neglecting the children and me. Anger was a new emotion for me. Before therapy, I saw myself as having little value, so I didn't think I was allowed to have negative feelings. Sal continued to meet our needs financially. But emotionally, he wasn't there for the children or me. I knew he was missing a lot of joy by not sharing in the kid's lives, but he didn't seem to care and I was helpless to do anything about it.

I would have to make a life for myself. I realized I couldn't physically leave Sal. Where could I go with all those children? I would simply have to make a life for myself, even though we still occupied the same house.

It had always been my desire to be involved in a political decision making role. But, Sal had discouraged me from doing anything outside of the home. Now I felt I had the freedom to do what I wanted, so I decided to run for election to the school board. I'm not sure whether my motives were completely altruistic, or if I just wanted to prove to Sal that I was a person of worth.

In any case, I was elected. At first the school superintendent was not very happy with me. I had defeated a long-time friend of his. During my first year on the board he didn't so much as address me by name. I was the only woman among nine members. The Superintendent called all the men by their first names, but he called me young lady. I felt patronized by him and most of the other men. Thank God I had two allies on the board who were supportive of me.

The Lord used me powerfully in at least two instances. The first was when some disgruntled clergymen objected to Christian ministers using the name of Jesus Christ when they were invited to give the benediction at high school graduation ceremonies. The principal of the high school came to the board to express this complaint. He asked us for a resolution to ban clergy from using the name Jesus Christ.

I became quite indignant and spoke strongly against such a prohibition. I persuaded the board to table the vote. The next day a newspaper reporter who had been covering the meeting wrote an account of the principal's request. The headline of her article read, "No Room for Jesus at North Brunswick High School." She mentioned my strong objection to the request and quoted me at length. The next Sunday, Father Crupi, the priest of the largest church in the area, publicly commended me for my stand and urged his parishioners to go to the next board meeting and support me.

There was an unusually large turnout for that meeting and many in the crowd spoke against the censoring of the clergy. The board compromised by voting to invite more than one clergy to participate in graduation ceremonies so that those who felt uncomfortable with prayer "in the name of Jesus" would also be represented.

In another incident a woman who called herself a "white witch" wanted to teach a course called, "Everything You Wanted to Know About the Occult but Were Afraid to Ask," at the adult evening school. I believed strongly that the school should not be teaching about the occult.

Once more, it was Phyllis to the rescue. This time there was a big brouhaha. The newspapers made an even bigger case of this. Much to my embarrassment a picture of eight-year-old daughter, Elena, dressed as a witch appeared in the same paper mentioned earler. She and a friend were putting together a Halloween Haunted House. I was totally unaware of the project. They went about the neighborhood dressed as witches, inviting the other kids to come. When they got to the home of the editor of the local paper, he snapped her picture and ... voila!

It came down to the issue of censorship and my right as a member of the board to influence the rest of the board. This issue prompted the local radio station to have a live debate between Ms. White Witch and me. There was also a call-in for listeners to present their views. It was a volatile evening to say the least. Because of all the publicity, I was invited to lecture on the subject of censorship at Rutgers State University.

When the time came to vote on whether or not the class should be approved, I really didn't have the majority of the board on my side. However, the night the vote was taken there were not enough members present to gather the majority needed for the class to be approved. I scored a technical knockout on that one.

I served for nine very rewarding years on the board. I grew to consider myself a person of worth in spite of my husband's rejection.

CHAPTER **XXVIII**

My Dad's Turn

*I*n 1970 something happened that would affect my family forever. After thirty-six years of an unhappy marriage, my dad and stepmother divorced. He hit bottom. He drank, gambled and womanized more than ever. A business associate intervened when he saw dad's downward spiral. He was a member of the Mennonite Church, which loved the Jews. Befriending my dad, he took every opportunity to tell him about the Messiah. He kept offering him a New Testament, but dad always refused. One day he became annoyed with his associate's persistence and said, "Leave me alone. If Jesus is truly the Messiah, I will find him in my Old Testament Scriptures."

That night dad went home and began pouring over the Scriptures. Like a man obsessed, he read night and day. What he first realized from his research was that the patriarchs of the Old Testament, the ones he held in holy esteem like Jacob, Isaac and King David, were often liars and connivers. This was an astonishing revelation to him. Those men were just like he was, far from perfect.

After one long, sleepless night of mulling things over in his mind, he fell on his knees and prayed this prayer, "God, if you could use those rascals I have been reading about in the Scriptures, maybe you could change me and use me. If you are the Jewish Messiah the Scriptures foretold, forgive me and change me."

My Jewish dad asked Jesus to be his Messiah!

When he arose, he knew beyond a shadow of a doubt he was forgiven and that Jesus was, indeed, the long-awaited Jewish Messiah. Jesus welcomed him with open arms. At sixty-five, my dad gave God his shattered and out-of-control life and God made a merciful exchange. He gave him a new life. My dad was radically and completely changed. He was born again, a new creature in Christ Jesus. He looked differently, he acted differently, and he talked differently. He even smelled differently. Gone was the odor of whiskey.

He was so excited about his salvation, that he continually talked about his Messiah, Y'shua. In fact, I thought he was going crazy or getting senile. I had been in the church for twenty-five years. I was Mrs. Super Catholic. Didn't I raise twelve children? Didn't I obey all the laws of the church? Yet, he had the audacity to tell me, "All your good deeds are like filthy rags!"

He really made me angry. I didn't act like he was acting and I didn't know anyone else who was so excited about God. He told me he was praying for my family and me to know Jesus as he did. At first I was indignant because he thought I needed his prayers; but, in my heart I knew he was acting out of love.

The three oldest sons, Rich, Tom, and Peter, were heavily involved in the hippie culture in the early seventies. Drugs, rock and roll, and girls were all they cared about. School, church, and family held no interest for them. The three boys went to Woodstock and other weekend concerts where they got wasted together. Tommy passed out on the beach in Florida after partying and woke up with second-degree burns all over his body.

I didn't know what to do. They were out of my control and there was nothing I could do about it. I felt I had not only failed as a wife, but now I was failing as a mother. And, to top it off, I was a drunk! It was probably the worst time in my life. I couldn't accept that I had indeed, failed in the most important areas of my life. I felt I had mishandled my life so badly that I didn't even deserve to live.

Though I had improved with therapy, I still thought I had value only if I were perfect. Foolishly, I thought killing myself was the perfect answer. What I hoped to accomplish, I don't know. One night, after drinking heavily, I got in my car determined to end it all by driving head-on into a tree. The tree loomed before me. But, at the last minute something stopped me, and I swerved.

I took a week's vacation to get myself together, and visited my dad in Florida. He had three *Tomberg's Rotisserie Chicken* stores in West Palm Beach. They had become famous for his special chicken, as well as Jewish foods such as chopped liver, potato pancakes, chicken soup and matzo balls. To spend time with him, I had to peel onions and cut up vegetables with him as he worked at a store.

I noticed he listened only to Christian radio stations in his home and at his businesses. Little by little as I worked alongside him, I started to pay attention to what the speakers on the radio were saying. I asked him a lot of tough questions. Seeds of a new life were being planted in my heart that week.

A year after he became a Christian, Dad married Vondale, a woman who worked for him. She was quite a bit younger than he was, but they appeared to love each other.

My three brothers, who lived in the same area in Florida, were angry with him when he divorced their mother, even though the marriage had failed long ago. They thought Vondale was the cause of the divorce. They were even more upset when Dad became a Christian.

He was a great source of embarrassment to them as he drove around town in his big brown Chrysler bearing large magnetic signs that read, "My Boss is a Jewish Carpenter" and "Jesus is My Messiah." He had also installed tract racks in each store to distribute leaflets discussing The Messiah, Jesus and Judaism. In the Christian community he was much admired for his bold witness.

He had grasped the concept that Jesus had come first for the Jews, then the Gentiles. He would recount this to his Jewish customers who questioned why he had tracts in his store. "He is our Messiah, not their Messiah," he would say.

105

His Jewish customers were wary and one time picketed his stores for what they considered proselytizing tactics. However, his customers, Jewish and otherwise, could not resist his delicious chicken and other dishes for long, and business continued to boom.

When a Jew becomes a Christian, it is considered a terrible thing in the Jewish community, a betrayal. Dad seemed to flaunt this betrayal as he drove around town with his Jews for Jesus billboard car. Since my brothers shared the Tomberg name and were well known businessmen in the community, my dad's outspoken conversion was quite distressing for them. It was especially painful when people described their father as a wonderful Christian. All these things caused a severance in their relationship. He was deeply grieved, but he could not deny his Messiah or stop witnessing for Him. Only my sister, Sandy, who is the most loving and kind woman I know, maintained a relationship with him.

Back home with my family, Rich, Tom and Peter, sporting long hair, torn jeans and guitars over their backs, were becoming more and more alienated from the family. Then in 1974, miracle of miracles, one after another they surrendered their lives to Jesus. Their looks didn't change much but, like my father, their lifestyles and attitudes were altogether different. They were totally changed. Instead of rock concerts, they went to church and Bible studies. And like their grandfather, they too talked about Jesus all the time.

The most obvious hallmark of these new Christians was the peace and joy they seemed to have found. I wanted what they had. These were things I desperately needed. What was going on? I was completely confused. First, my dad's changed life, and now, my sons. Could I have the same changes in my life?

I went to church and diligently followed every precept of the church. Why didn't I have their joy and peace? I became involved in more religious activities, but I didn't find peace. I took college courses. They were challenging, but that for which I yearned still eluded me. I spoke to our priest and told him I needed something more, but he had no answers for me. All the while, I was drinking heavily, mired in guilt and shame.

CHAPTER XXIX

Word of Life

Dad and Vondale would drive up from Florida to attend Word of Life Christian Camp at Scroon Lake in upstate New York each year. He would invite the younger children and me to come along as his guests for a week long vacation. I always refused.

I imagined everyone at that camp would be straight-laced and look like the American gothic painting of the stern-faced farmer with the pitchfork and his equally stern faced wife. What would I have in common with them? It didn't seem to me that it would be much of a vacation. I smoked, drank and loved to dance. I didn't see how I could have any fun at a Christian camp.

Still, Dad would invite us. After four years of refusing, I ran out of excuses and said I would go. Monica, Raphael, Debbie, and Elena went with us. My first impression when we arrived was that everyone looked normal. I didn't see any straight-laced American gothic types. The campgrounds were beautiful. A wonderful sense of tranquility seemed to permeate the entire facility.

The children stayed on an island in the middle of a lake and had their own camp. The adults stayed at a beautiful inn. Maybe this isn't going to be so bad after all, I thought.

We were assigned different tables for dinner each evening and one of the men at the table would pray before we ate. The words were beautiful, like no prayers I had ever heard. They prayed as though they personally knew the One to whom they were speaking. One night I sneaked a peek as one of the men prayed, thinking he must have the prayer written on his shirt cuff. I couldn't believe they were spontaneous.

Each night after dinner there was a speaker. The week I attended, there was a well-known speaker on eschatology, which is end times prophecy. More than once he referred to the Catholic Church as the whore of Babylon. I was hopping mad! Here I had come all this way as a favor to Dad, and my church was being insulted. How dare he?

After he finished speaking about Jesus and the end times he would issue an invitation and ask those who wanted Jesus to be their Savior to come up front. Only a few responded, because almost everyone at the camp was already a Christian. When those who did respond returned to their seats, I could see they had been touched. Some had tears on their cheeks, others had a smile on their lips. Evidently something had happened, but what?

I was still angry with the speaker and I surmised there was some kind of mind control being used. Since I had such a lofty opinion of my intellectual prowess, I knew those things wouldn't work on me. Still, I couldn't ignore the obvious peace and joy that prevailed among the other campers. They were the same attitudes I saw in my dad and my three oldest sons. I knew it was tied somehow to an understanding of Jesus that I didn't have. I was determined to find out what it was and how I could have it also, in spite of Dwight Pentecost, the Catholic basher.

I made a deal with God. "God," I said, "if You send someone here more intelligent than I and they believe in this Jesus stuff and can explain it to me, maybe I can believe also." I had an attitude of superiority about my intelligence. The very next night, much to my amazement, God put me at a dinner table with a Christian psychiatrist! God loved me enough to answer my plea. I asked Dr. Belikias if I could perhaps talk with him. He was more than happy to indulge me, and we made an appointment for the next afternoon.

I was eager to have the peace and joy I saw in the Christians around me and I told him that this was what I was desperately seeking. He asked me if I read the Bible. I told him I knew some passages, but I had never really read it. He said the answers for my life could be found in that Book. For the next four hours he took me on a whirlwind tour of God's Word. We started at Genesis and finished with Revelation. What a trip that was! It took me from here to eternity.

As Dr. Belikias read me Scripture passages from the Old Testament, I realized the great love and hope God had for His creation. Beginning in the Garden of Eden, man's willful disobedience became apparent. Yet, surprisingly, though each generation alternately obeyed and disobeyed God, He never relinquished His love and hope for man.

As we went further into the study, I became more and more awed by the holiness of God, and more aware of my sinfulness. The Ten Commandments revealed that I had not kept at least five of them. I felt convicted that even though I thought I was obeying God by keeping all the rules and regulations of my church, in truth I was a sinner.

But, God knew this all the time. I think He allowed me to live under the law to show me that the law does not save us or give us hope. As Dr. Belikias walked me through the centuries with my Jewish forefathers, I saw my life mirrored in theirs. They, as I, tried to keep the law, but their human weaknesses and penchant toward sin made it impossible. And then, I heard these dramatic words,

"When the fullness of time was come, God sent forth His Son, made of a woman, made under the law, to redeem them that were under the law, that we might receive the adoption of sons" (Galatians 4:4-5).

"God so loved the world, that he gave his only begotten Son, that whosoever believeth in him should not perish, but have everlasting life" (John 3:16).

"For the wages of sin is death; but the gift of God is eternal life through Jesus Christ our Lord" (Romans 6:23).

It was incomprehensible to me that Jesus, the Son of God, paid with His life so that I could spend eternity in heaven with Him. Contrary to what I thought, I could not earn my way into heaven. It mattered not how many church services I attended, how often I fasted, or how well I obeyed the Church's rules and regulations. I may have been a very religious as a Catholic, but I didn't have a relationship with Christ.

Finally, Dr. Belikias inquired if I would like to ask Jesus to be my Savior and Lord. I somehow knew my life would change if I did so. I had lived it my way. I had tried to control every situation by lying, crying, denying, or whatever it took to ensure I was in control. Now, I would be relinquishing that control to Jesus.

I asked, "How will I know how to live this new life?"

He told me that as soon as I asked Jesus to be my Lord and Savior, the Holy Spirit would come to guide and direct me. "Oh, so that is what the Holy Ghost is all about!" I thought.

I wanted, more than I had ever wanted anything, all that was so apparent in my dad, my sons and the people at the camp. If it was Jesus that gave them such peace, then I wanted Him. I took that leap of faith and asked Jesus to be my Lord and Savior. I felt like I was jumping off a cliff, leaving everything behind. I didn't know if I could live this new life, letting God control my life, to which I desperately clung. Dr. Belikias told me to confess my sins and the Lord would forgive me and set me free.

Very quietly I did just that.

That afternoon, I began what is the rest and best part of my life. When I asked Jesus to be my Savior on August 7, 1975, I became aware of the journey that God has been taking me on towards the Promised Land.

Twenty years after I accepted the Lord I was impressed to write a note to Jack Wirtzen and thank him for the crucial part Word of Life played in my conversion and my children's lives. The four youngest kids who were with me that week were also saved at the camp. I am glad I obeyed God's leading to write when I did, because two weeks later Mr. Wirtzen went to his eternal reward.

When I was baptized a Catholic twenty-five years previously, I was told I was a convert—no longer a Jew. Now I realized that other Christians treated my Jewish birth as a great, privileged birth. They said now that I knew my Messiah, I was a "completed Jew." As time went on and I learned more of the Bible, and saw what an important role the Jews played in both the Old and New Testament: I began for perhaps the first time to embrace my Jewish roots. I understood what my grandparents meant when they said being Jewish was special because we were God's chosen people.

CHAPTER XXX

Growing Pains

My father was very happy that the children and I had accepted the Messiah. But, no less than we were. I wish I could say that immediately upon asking Jesus to be my Lord and Savior, my struggles ended and my life instantly became wonderful. It is seldom that way! Truth be told, becoming a mature Christian is not instantaneous, but rather a process. As was my case, old things do pass away, but not always immediately.

At a particularly vulnerable time in my life when Sal was not interested in me as a woman, I met a man who seemed at the time to be everything Sal wasn't. He made me laugh, he was an intellectual, and he absolutely adored me. He thought I was the greatest. The rejection I was experiencing from my husband made this other man's traits irresistibly seductive.

He was married as well and we both knew a fling was not going to become a permanent relationship. I had deluded myself into thinking that since my husband had rejected me and we weren't hurting anyone, I was free to be in this relationship. I allowed my emotions to rule me, instead of the Word of God.

One night I came home and went to my bedroom. There was Sal in bed, bloated from drinking and snoring away. The room reeked of alcohol and cigarette smoke. As I looked at him in this terrible state, this Scripture came into my mind, "Thy desire shall be to thy husband" (Gen. 3:16b).

It was true! Sal was my husband and the only man I loved and desired. No matter how I tried to rationalize my extra-marital affair, God convicted me that it was purely and simply adultery, which is sin. It didn't matter what Sal did and didn't do. That was between him and God. But, I was bound by the Scriptural commandment "Thou shall not commit adultery."

I ended the sinful relationship. It wasn't easy, but I knew I had no choice if I wanted to live a life pleasing to God. Sin may be enjoyable for a season, but remorse can last a lifetime. I know God has forgiven me, but I wish I had never lived that season of my life.

When I became a Christian, I thought I was the only adult in my community who knew the Lord until I started to attend a ladies Bible study at the local Baptist Church. Only then did I learn there were many other Christians in my town.

At first, I attempted to become a clone of other Christians, especially when I attended charismatic services with my older children. I raised my hands when they did, albeit self-consciously. I said, "Praise the Lord" and clapped when they did. I was not used to that much enthusiasm and I felt terribly self-conscious.

Meanwhile, I continued to attend the Catholic Church. Little by little I realized their doctrine did not mesh with the Scriptures I had started to read. I had been told at Word of Life that this would happen. Yet, I didn't feel a release to leave the Church until one day God sent me a message via the Holy Spirit. He simply said, "You are free to leave."

My daughter, Diane, and her husband were then attending a very friendly church, which I had visited. It was called Liberty Tabernacle. The pastor was I.D. Bird, a former Baptist minister. Pastor Bird had been filled with the Holy Spirit while he was recuperating from heart surgery. His denomination did not appreciate his talking about divine healing and speaking in tongues. He was asked to vacate his pulpit. Soon he became an itinerant revival preacher. As he went from church to church he gathered a group of followers who urged him to pastor them.

He began holding Sunday meetings in the farmhouse in which he lived. Every Sunday there was a potluck dinner after service. His congregation became known as "the church that eats." Going to these church meetings became a joyful time I looked forward to each Sunday. I loved the contemporary worship and spontaneity of people speaking out as the Lord inspired them. It was an exciting time for me as I learned the Bible and more about what it meant to be part of a New Testament Church.

I grew by leaps and bounds. Pastor Bird was an excellent Bible teacher and many people in the church were also very learned in the Scriptures, setting a good example as they quoted from them. I soon became an avid student of the Word of God and before long I memorized many verses.

Some of my children attended church with me, and although Raphael was very young at the time, he became an integral member of the worship team along with Plinky. I urged Sal to attend with us, telling him what fun we had.

His reply, "Church is not supposed to be fun, it is supposed to fulfill an obligation." Even though he had stopped going to Sunday mass, he said, "The Catholic Church is the only true church."

By 1978 Raphael was witnessing to his friends at school through the Christian songs he wrote and played during lunch break each day. He and other young Christians would witness to their peers at the local shopping center. There was a Video Game Center there, which became fertile ground for the promotion of the Gospel.

The owner was himself almost persuaded to become a Christian. This was a time of visitation by the Holy Spirit and many young people came to the Lord. The young people would question Raphael about theology which he wasn't sure how to answer. So, he would say, "Ask my Mom."

Soon there were kids, hungry for God in our home at all hours of the day. I decided it would be much better to have a regular Bible study for young people once a week. This became the largest movement of God among young people North Brunswick ever experienced.

Our good friends, Vince and Kathy Cata, were having Saturday evening fellowship in their home with many young people attending. That was in Metuchen, however, about twelve miles from North Brunswick. It seemed we needed something like that locally.

CHAPTER **XXXI**

The North Brunswick Fellowship

I began a regular Monday evening meeting in our home. I would often enlist Bible teachers to come and minister to the group. They would be amazed at the zeal and fervor of the group. It was undeniable that the Holy Spirit was doing a new thing among us.

Raphael led worship and we often had four other guitarists providing worship music. Young people would come from miles around as the word of these meetings spread. I felt ill-prepared to minister to the group that had now grown to about forty. I thought a man should be in charge; but none came forth.

Yet, I felt the Lord directing me to provide snacks and deliver the message He gave me. As the group grew in number so did the many cars and pickup trucks parked in and around our driveway. Sal was not happy about this. I knew I needed to find another meeting place, but I kept putting it off until Sal finally left a sign on the piano announcing that this evening's meeting was going to be the last in our home.

What would I do? I had to find a new home for The North Brunswick Youth Fellowship, popularly known as "Monday Night." I approached the elders of Georges Road Baptist Church and they agreed to let us use the church facilities on Monday evenings. The kindness of this church overwhelmed me.

After a month's hiatus, we started meeting in this church. I was not sure anyone would come because most of the young people who attended were unchurched and I was afraid an actual church building would scare them away. But it didn't. Before long the group more than doubled and we had close to one hundred coming out each week.

The age range was thirteen to thirty. We made no pretension of establishing a church, though there was much encouragement to do so. Yet, because most of the group was unchurched, I knew it was important to teach New Testament Church principles such as living holy lives, telling others about Jesus, and serving and giving to those in need.

Our group bore little resemblance to the average church youth group. In appearance most of the young people looked like they were part of the heavy metal pop culture. They wore leather, sported spiked hair and spiked jewelry. But, these young people came in droves because God drew them and placed a hunger to know Him in their hearts.

We didn't have icebreakers and the usual fun and games. Instead we had worship that often lasted an hour. Applying biblical principles to their daily lives was the major thrust. Body ministry was emphasized as we prayed for each other. Then we would have a time of fellowship. Granted, many came to meet other young people. At least three strong marriages came out of the group.

I did not want the group to be known as the Phyllis and Raphael Giglio group. As soon as I could, I asked others to share in leadership. Vince and Kathy Cata gave up their Saturday meetings and joined forces with us, providing wonderful help in leading and teaching. Eventually Andrea Calabretta, Jimmy Di Paola and Mark Salerno, each gifted in leadership, joined Vince, Cathy, Raphael and me, to comprise our leadership team.

Youth With A Mission, a para-church group known as YWAM, provided many gifted speakers such as Leland Paris. They also gave our group opportunities for discipleship training and short-term and long-term missions trips in which many of us participated. Andrea served in England and Africa with YWAM. Raphael and Mark Salerno participated in an Olympic torch run across the country, carrying not only the torch, but the gospel as well.

We crossed every denominational barrier. Vineyard Churches were springing up at the time. Leaders such as Mike Turrigiano from that group came and taught us about the gifts of the Holy Spirit and most especially about divine healing. Dana Morey, who had worked with Campus Crusade, came from Chicago and taught coping skills based on the Bible. Bob Turton, an officer with American Rescue Workers, taught about serving. J.E. Caterson, a CMA pastor, shared his experiences as a missionary with us. Harry Thomas, the founder of the Creation Festivals, was a frequent speaker. My son, Tom, was one of our retreat speakers. There were many others who came and shared their hearts with us.

Most importantly, lives were changed. We had found favor with God. He chose to pour out His Spirit and kids were getting saved and being set free from destructive lifestyles. Ironically, when Jewish kids came to our meetings and realized that Jesus could deliver them from alcohol and drug use, and they made a decision to follow Jesus; their parents became angry. It seems the drugs and alcohol abuse they could tolerate, but Jesus? Never! "Not in my house will you be born again!"

After two years our group was asked to stop meeting in the church. Some irate elders did not want "those kids" to give their church a bad name. Some of the kids smoked and cigarette butts were noticed at the door. Some unmarried moms brought their babies and put them to sleep in the nursery. Never mind that this was the only outreach to the community the church had.

My heart broke when I was given the news and I could not stop crying. It was not a pity party; it was a deep sorrow for the church. The decision to ask us to leave was by no means unanimous and some people left the church because of the elders' decision.

This happened on the Monday before Thanksgiving. Though I did not attend this church, I planned to go to the Thanksgiving service and express my thanks to those people for their hospitality. The still, small voice of the Holy Spirit spoke to me and said, "Go to the Thanksgiving Day service, because if you don't, bitterness will come into your heart and you will never want to enter this church again." That was some of the best counsel I ever received and I am glad I obeyed.

Fifteen years later one of the elders came to me when I was speaking at the same church and asked my forgiveness for his part in our group being asked to leave. It was a beautiful moment as we reconciled and hugged each other.

I was serving on the school board at the time we were asked to stop meeting at the church. I asked the superintendent in charge of buildings if we could use a storeroom in the board office building for our meetings. His wonderful reply was, "Why don't you meet at the high school?"

The Bible tells us that, "God is able to do over and above anything we can hope or ask or think" (Ephesians 3:20). I never would have presumed we could meet at the high school.

For the next four years we had extraordinary meetings at the high school! When the weather allowed, we met in an outdoor amphitheater. When the weather was bad, we met in the teacher's lunchroom. Our group grew tremendously during that time, both spiritually and in numbers. We usually had a hundred or more people coming.

One of the activities we were involved in were summertime trips to the New Jersey shore and having a time of worship on the beach or boardwalk. The young people leading worship were excellent musicians and they always drew a large crowd. After the music we would have a time of testimony and witnessing. This was a natural outgrowth of our fellowship. This was the Holy Spirit working through His children.

Chapter XXXII

Looking Beyond Ourselves

One week before Christmas in 1984, I, with a group of young people from the fellowship, left my comfortable suburban home and the maddening mall-mania of Christmas and boarded a plane for Mexico. Under the auspices of Calvary Commission's Mexico Christmas Outreach, our purpose was to bring to needy people the Good News of Jesus, along with gifts of food, clothing and toys. Our destination was Ramos, Mexico, where the poorest of the poor lived.

I was aware of a great need in my own life to live out the message of the gospel. It was increasingly possible for me to major in the minors of Christianity, such as church politics and other trappings of organized religion. I was too easily forgetting the major issues, such as loving my neighbor. God used the precious people of Ramos to teach me some things I pray I will never forget.

Geographically, the people of Ramos are close neighbors. They are only a few miles from the airport in McAllen, Texas, near the Mexican border.

Socio-economically they could be any Third-World countries, thousands of miles away. The Bible tells me I am to love my neighbor as myself. There is little doubt that I love my family and myself. The challenge for me was to discover what God would have me do to love the people of Ramos in the same way I love myself.

Most of the children in Ramos have no fathers. Some have no mothers. Some of the mothers are prostitutes and have gone elsewhere to ply their trade, leaving their kids behind in Ramos. Who cares for these kids and how do they survive? Only by God's grace it seems. Scripture says, "When my mother and father desert me the Lord will lift me up." The children we saw did not appear to be starving.

Mexican people love children, their own as well as others. Though the people of Ramos are extremely poor and have a hard time caring for their own families, they also provide for these children without homes. Unfortunely, the children looked like they had not had a bath in a long time. Their clothing was ragged. Some had no shoes. Many of them had bad coughs, runny noses and poor color. Considering their living conditions, this was not surprising.

The average home in Ramos is a poorly constructed one-room shack. The furnishings are extremely sparse, with one bed the whole family sleeps in and perhaps a table and chair. There is no indoor plumbing, and for some, no electricity. The cooking is done on an open fire outdoors.

Imagine housekeeping with no utilities at all. Life in Ramos is like a perpetual backwoods camping trip. Even their water is purchased from a vendor who comes around in a horse drawn wagon. The streets are unpaved and rutted. When it rains they become rivers of mud. There is very little beauty to take away the bleakness of the environment. Perhaps the only beauty there is found in the faces of the children.

Josues pastors the people of Ramos. The building they use for church is the former brothel and bar. It is completely gutted and empty except for some homemade benches that serve as pews. There is no electric or any other convenience. The floor is dirt. The place smells as though it also doubles as a public toilet, and no amount of disinfectant can cover that odor. Yet, the people have a hunger for God and come whenever services are held.

One day, I asked the leader of our group how the children of Ramos escape from this poverty and the deprivation of even basic needs. How can they hope for a brighter future? "Only through Jesus," he replied.

Later that day the young people and I visited some of the homes to invite the people to the "church" where we would be distributing toys and food.

We could see a real difference between those who said they were Christians and those who did not know the Lord. The homes of the Christians were much cleaner and there was a sparkle in their eyes. It became apparent to all of us that afternoon that a relationship with Jesus really does make a difference. Christians shine as lights in a dark place.

God has placed a great love in my heart for Ramos and especially for the children. I have seen the situation, and the Holy Spirit has filled me with compassion for these kids. I know that except for the grace of God, it could be me struggling to raise my children in a one-room shack in Ramos. The young people I took with me said they would never be the same after that mission trip.

On fire to witness and serve after the mission trip, we held weekend retreats at America's Keswick and Harvey Cedars each year. More young people were saved and received deliverance from ungodly habits. There was also a nursing home ministry. During one of the visits, a couple visiting their relative were so impressed with our group they asked who we were, and then came to our next meeting. When the offering was taken, this couple put in a check for $1,200.00. This money was used to repair and paint a young widow's house. All the work was done by the fellowship.

A prison ministry also sprung up, led by one of the alumnus of the prison who was a leader in our group. We picketed at abortion clinics, saving at least one baby's life, and were able to provide support, housing and financial assistance to the mother and her child. Some of the older ones in our group started an outreach to punk rockers hanging out in bars. We had open-mike nights just for people to share what God was doing in their lives. But, more than anything else we did, we worshipped the living God.

There was no paid staff, we owned no buildings, and we had no budget. In the truest sense, we were a church built not by human hands but by God and the Holy Spirit maintained us. We hoped it would go on forever, but it lived for only seven vibrant years.

By God's sovereign will it began and by God's sovereign will it ended in 1986. I will always be grateful to God for the privilege of serving Him through this group.

I continued with the tradition of having a Christ-centered Passover Seder. This had been a yearly event in the fellowship. As a Messianic Jew I loved to celebrate my Jewish heritage and share it with others. Often in the fellowship, we would follow the Seder with foot washing just as Jesus did after He celebrated the Passover Seder (The Last Supper) with His disciples.

Each year, more and more people young and old, attended. As we broke the unleavened bread along with the Bread of Life, the truth of the messianic message brought new enlightenment. As the Messianic Haggadah (Hebrew order of ceremony) points out, Jesus is very visible all through the Passover. It is only because satan has blinded the eyes of our Jewish brethren that they do not see it. God gave me many opportunities to share the Passover in local churches, including a Japanese church that loved the Jewish people.

Our fellowship has had a couple wonderful reunions, but I look forward to the big reunion in heaven when we can all meet again with all whose lives were touched by God through a fellowship called Monday Night.

CHAPTER XXXIII

A New Season

The season of the North Brunswick Fellowship ended and though there were valiant efforts to bring it back to life, it was not to be. For a while I felt like I had lost my identity since I was no longer a leader. Pride is a tenacious sin. I missed being somebody important. But, it seemed that God was putting me on the shelf.

By 1975 my father, brothers and sister all lived in Florida. I did not get to see my sister and brothers very often. Though it was never discussed, my dad's Christianity pretty much alienated him from my brothers. Dad was not invited to their children's weddings, bar Mitzvahs and the like. Only my sister, Sandy, a very special lady, came to visit him.

Dad had become a patriarch to all my family. He became the husband, father, grandfather and great-grandfather God meant him to be when he became a Christian. He dispensed advice and practical wisdom seasoned with humor and love.

My kids and their families loved to visit him. Of course, he always put them to work on a building or fix-up project, but they did not mind. One time I called him when my son Tom, his wife, Jean and their children were visiting him. I asked, "So, Dad how are you enjoying your grandkids?" He thought for a moment and replied, "What I am really enjoying is the great grandkids. You see, I forgot a lot of what I used to know and they don't know too much, so we get along wonderfully."

He was always the optimist. His favorite saying first thing in the morning when he saw you was, "Well, God gave you another day; if you messed up yesterday, do better today." When I would ask him how he slept the night before, he would say, "I slept like a baby: up an hour, cried an hour." Or he might answer, "Don't know. I was sleeping."

Dad's health started failing when he turned eighty. He had insufficiency of the heart to pump blood and he also had a mild form of leukemia. His mind, however, was as sharp as ever. He was a great card player. Pinochle had been his game. Some in his church didn't approve of "cards," so he stopped. Skipbo, a family card game like Uno, was acceptable and now that was his game.

I visited him about once a month and every weekend visit contained at least four games of Skipbo. All of my family got hooked on it. When dad died, my sons, who knew how Grandpa had loved the RBC's publication, "My Daily Bread," and the Skipbo game, put the cards and a booklet in his coffin.

Just before he died, he had a dream. In it, he was running for exercise. He had a towel around his neck to absorb the sweat that flowed from every pore. As he ran he felt like a young man full of vitality and life. When he ran back to his house, he dreamt he saw his wife, Vondale, thirty years his junior, cooking at the stove. In reality, she was a very strong youthful-looking woman. In his dream she looked old and shriveled up. He realized he had been given a foretaste of what the next life would be like.

From that dream, he received the assurance that no matter how young and strong we may appear to be in this life, we are all made of corruptible flesh that is dying. But God promises us that in heaven we will have a new body, made of incorruptible flesh that will never die and we will be forever young.

As he had grown weaker and more tired toward the end, he would say, "I am willing to stay, but I am ready to go."

About a year before his death he asked me to accompany him to a funeral home to make his final arrangements. A smartly dressed woman answered the door. She introduced herself; I introduced myself; then Dad introduced himself, "How do you do, I am Saul Tomberg, the participant."

From the look that passed over the woman's face, it was obvious that no "future customer"' had introduced himself or herself in that manner. He knew his going home was drawing near and his prayer was that no matter what or how his end would come, he would maintain his Christian witness and show forth God's grace. Neither did he want to become a burden to his wife and family.

God was very gracious to him. One morning he awakened, got into the shower, slipped and fell, and entered Heaven's portals. I rejoiced when Vondale called me with the news. I knew he died the way he wished—quickly. My grieving came later.

At his funeral I had the privilege of eulogizing him. I was able to share the Gospel and tell of Dad's love for his family and for Jesus. My brothers and sisters came and I had the opportunity to tell them how he grieved over his estrangement from them, but how he could not deny his faith in Jesus Christ.

Ironically Dad's death brought life. It made a way for all of his children and children's children to resume our relationships with each other. Since his death, we have had great family reunions. I know this is something he had longed for and somehow I believe he is smiling at us.

Chapter XXXIV

When You Come to the End of Your Rope There is Hope

I n the months after Dad's death I realized what a bulwark of strength he had become for me. I had come to depend on his wisdom. Many times I picked up the phone to call him for advice, or just to chat, and then came the stark realization he was no longer there. It was during this time that I realized my dad had become for me what my husband wasn't. As long as I had him to confide in, it didn't matter that Sal was not available to me.

So, I asked God to help me work on my marriage. Sal agreed that our relationship was not what it should be, but he rejected my pleas that we seek counseling. I decided to seek professional help alone. In my mind I assumed there were only two solutions to our difficulties. They were to divorce or grin and bear it. Neither of these was acceptable. I approached the counseling sessions with the mindset that Sal was the villain and I was the long-suffering, wronged heroine.

Much to my surprise and chagrin, I discovered a lot about me that wasn't pretty. I needed to make some changes. I discovered that the unforgiveness I bore towards Sal had been tainting my marriage. I thought I had forgiven him when I became a Christian. But, I had just "stuffed" my negative feelings, thinking that was forgiveness.

They hadn't gone away. These feelings would resurface, disguised as something else like anger, depression or illness.

After much counseling I realized I needed to go to my husband and, with a loving attitude, completely and specifically forgive him. I also had to ask his forgiveness for the many wrong things I had done. As I learned the true meaning of forgiveness, I realized how wrong I had been. I had to take full responsibility before God and before my husband for my wrongdoing without excuses. God doesn't forgive excuses, he forgives sin.

I also learned what Biblical submission is. I thought it was hard to submit to an unsaved husband. I submitted not because I wanted to, but because the Bible said I had to. I learned I could choose to submit. This was a whole different approach. I gained a new way of looking at things through the counseling.

It was very frightening to me to think about going back and opening the door to the room where all the hurts were stored and reliving the episodes that had nearly destroyed me. Fortunately, the counselor had chosen for me to read *The Marriage Builder* by Dr. Larry Crabb[2].

In the book, Dr. Crabb presents a chalkboard sketch of a woman standing on the edge of a precipice looking into a deep, dark valley. Around her waist is a loosely-tied rope. Above her, high in the clouds unseen by her, is the hand of God holding the other end of the rope. As long as she stays where she is, she is not even conscious of the rope around her. But, if she were to descend into that valley, the rope would become taut and she would not be hurt. The interpretation is that this is how God's grace operates. You will not experience it until you need it. When you need it, you will feel it.

With trepidation I finally summoned the courage to go to Sal. I felt like the woman in the illustration. I was afraid he would reject what I was saying. I, too, was on the edge of a precipice looking down into the unknown. What would happen? Would my husband deny any wrongdoing? Would he minimize my efforts at reconciliation? I didn't know what the result would be and I could only pray it would be good.

I took the plunge. During a long car trip I brought the subject up. To my relief Sal took the matter very seriously and said he had done a lot of stupid things in the past and that he was sorry. I asked him to forgive me for my transgressions and he did. We talked a lot about our lives.

Since then, have we lived ecstatic, storybook happily-ever-after lives? Well, maybe not "ecstatical," but it was a place to start the healing.

In the Old Testament the prophet Samuel built an altar after a blessing from God. He named it Ebenezer, which in Hebrew means "stone of help."

He said, "thus far the Lord has helped us" (I Samuel 7:12). I would have liked to do the same on Route 539 in New Jersey because God was there and without His help reconciliation with Sal would not have been possible.

In 1997, we celebrated fifty years of marriage. Our kids gave us a party that was more like the wedding we never had. What a glorious day that was as we rejoiced with family and friends. We also renewed our wedding vows with four clergy present. Even our good friend the late Monsignor Crupi from the Italian Catholic Church prayed over us, along with Reverend Stephan Nash, Sr., Reverend Robert W. Cruver and Reverend J.E. Caterson.

To top it off our children gave us a fantastic trip to the Grand Canyon, which we will never ever forget. The majesty of what God had wrought held us in awe as we beheld the unbelievably magnificent rock formations and the deep crevices where the mighty Colorado River appears like a thin blue ribbon. The song, "How Great Thou Art," was constantly on my lips as we delighted in the breathtaking scenery.

I remember asking the Lord during a time of quiet contemplation as I sat on a rock ledge, "How can it be? How did we make it through all of the struggles and all of the ups and downs of fifty years of marriage?"

His reply was, "You did it one day at a time by my grace."

I wrote a poem for Sal for that Anniversary:

Looking Back—Looking Ahead

It seems like it was just yesterday when we said, "I do!"

You and I made that vow not knowing how little we knew.

We tied our lives together with words stronger then steel,

And we promised to stay together no matter how we would feel.

The years have been good to us. We've known God's grace.

He kept us safe for fifty years as we ran this race.

Today, again, I pledge my love, knowing so much more,

And I vow to stay by your side till we reach that other shore.

CHAPTER XXXV

Grandma Goes to College

aving been active all my life, I wasn't ready to settle into retirement mode, even though my children were now grown and out of the house. I had gained an enormous amount of experience with children and young people over the years. And, if there is one thing our Lord can use among those who are yielded to Him, it is the wisdom that comes from experience. He prodded me to press on.

I thought I might be suited for counseling others. So, I decided to take some counseling classes at Zarephath Bible Institute in Somerset County, New Jersey. The classes were terrific and I learned a great deal.

I had a problem with only one class. It was caused by what I will call a pride issue. The class was titled, "Child Rearing in the 90s." A twenty-eight-year-old father of a sixteen-month-old baby taught it. He thought he had all the answers based on his limited child-rearing experience.

It was very difficult to sit through those classes when I was the one with all the experience, having raised children in the 60s, 70s, 80s and 90s. If it hadn't been for my pride in my knowing better than the professor and constantly asserting myself, I might have enjoyed the class. Instead, I merely tolerated those weekend sessions.

However, once more I was made aware of God's constant grace at work. The final exam was to write a personal improvement plan consisting of our life story, including the mistakes we had made and our plans for improvement. God used the recounting of my life to bring me tremendous revelation and healing. It is amazing that, just as the Word says, "You shall know the truth and the truth shall set you free." That paper became the genesis of this book.

After I took all the counseling classes that were offered, I started attending Zarephath Bible Institute in 1989. I had as my goal a degree in Biblical Studies. Robert W. Cruver, a friend of Raphael's since they were teenagers, is president of the school. I had always loved this young man and sensed a deep spirituality in him. I wanted to support him and be an encouragement to him in the position that had been laid on his young shoulders: that of breathing new life into an old and honored institution.

I had a thirst for knowledge, especially about the Bible and Christianity. Soon after that I joined Zarephath Community Chapel. Right from the beginning I felt that the church and Zarephath Bible Institute were pregnant with the promise of great things to come. The Lord knows, I knew about being pregnant, and I wanted to be a part of it. Besides, I felt such tremendous peace each time I crossed the little Canal Bridge and drove onto the Zarephath campus.

Zarephath Bible Institute was established in 1908 by a woman with a vision and a widow with land who combined their gifts. They have been used of God, and have seen thousands of lives changed in this country and abroad.

"Child Rearing in the 90s" notwithstanding, I really enjoyed my studies. Whole new areas of enlightenment were provided to me as I sat under excellent teachers. As I came close to the time of matriculation, I realized I would have to take mathematics and biology classes in order to graduate.

I avoided both until the very last semester. I was hoping Jesus would return and I would be taken to heaven before I had to take those two classes. Alas, He did not. I wasn't too worried about the math class. I knew the teacher and his wife through a mentoring relationship. Both of them called me Mother. I thought he couldn't possibly fail his "Mother." He didn't, but neither did he cut me any slack. I barely made it through the class.

The biology class required a lot of memory work and I just could not remember the steps of cell division and so on. I took large amounts of the herb Ginko Biloba, which is supposed to improve the memory, but I was beyond help. Thankfully, part of the final exam was writing an essay on which I did well. Fortunately for me, the instructor exercised the gift of mercy and I passed that course, also. What bliss!

After ten years of taking classes I was ready to graduate. I was feeling very smug and proud of myself and what I had accomplished. Then, the Lord began to deal with me. I hate when that happens. In essence, this is what He said, "You think you're the cat's pajamas don't you, missy? You know you didn't pass those courses on your own, you made it through by My grace."

He was right, and all I could say was, "Thank you, Lord. Your Grace has been my portion throughout my life. On my own I can do nothing; but with Your grace, nothing is impossible."

My graduation was wonderful. Though I was sixty-eight years old, I felt like a kid again. I wore a cap and gown. My son, Peter, took a traditional post-graduation picture of me, tossing my cap in the air. A lot of my family and friends attended the ceremony. Then we had a big party back at our house with a cake and all the trimmings.

I shall never forget that day and the joy I felt as I walked down the aisle and received my diploma. Because I had left school to marry, graduating from college, however late, and receiving a diploma, was a very big deal for me.

CHAPTER XXXVI

Rhinestone Jesus

T he Lord has given me a wonderful ministry as a speaker for Christian Women's Clubs. This is part of Stonecroft Ministries. The purpose of the clubs is to provide a way for Christian women to bring their unsaved friends to a luncheon or dinner where they are fed, entertained, and presented with an inspirational message. The volunteers who chair these events are dedicated, praying women who work hard to produce an atmosphere that is non-threatening and fun.

My part as the speaker at these events is to share my testimony of what life was like before Christ, how I came to know Him and how my life has changed. I then give an invitation for anyone who has never done so to ask Jesus to be her Savior. What a blessed privilege I have had to be there as hundreds of women have responded.

To date, my travels have taken me to Pennsylvania, New York, Virginia, Connecticut and New Mexico. A fringe benefit of this ministry is that I often stay at the homes of families who provide gracious Christian hospitality. It has been a joy to get to know many wonderful people in this manner.

I marvel at the trust these good people place in me, since they sometimes have to leave for work before I leave their home. All they really know about me is that I am a Christian. And for them that is enough.

I have had some unique experiences as I travel. Last January I was invited to conduct a women's retreat in New Mexico. I was very excited to be doing this and delighted to visit the Southwest for the first time. The night before I left I e-mailed my family and asked them to pray for God's presence at the retreat, and to pray for me because I had to change planes in Atlanta. That airport is huge and can be overwhelming.

As I dressed for the trip the morning I left, I felt a nudge to dig out my rhinestone Jesus pin and wear it. I had purchased it about ten years ago in a moment of charismatic fervor. I loved it when I first bought it, but then after a while I considered it to be a bit flashy.

There it was, glittering at the bottom of my meager box of jewelry. Well, I obeyed the nudge and fastened the pin to my sweater and didn't give it another thought.

When we landed in Atlanta I got off the plane and made my way into the airport. Suddenly I heard, "Yes, Jesus is the way!" and, "Praise the Lord!"

The cheers were coming from two female passenger assistants who spotted or were bedazzled by my glittering pin. They were waiting with wheelchairs in case there was someone who needed assistance.

I walked over to them and we had a spontaneous thirty-second praise gathering. One of the girls asked where I was going and, in truth, I said, "I don't know."

I hadn't looked at what gate or plane I needed to take to complete the last leg of my journey.

She looked at my ticket and said, "Sit down in the chair, girl!"

I replied, "Oh, I am not disabled."

To which she very emphatically said, "I said, sit down in that chair, girl!"

I thought it could be God talking so I didn't argue. I sat down and off we went. My trip took me on an elevator, down a hall, on a tram, then a long ride to my gate. I think those girls were angels assigned by God to take care of me. He told them, "You will know her because she will be the only one at the Atlanta Airport wearing a rhinestone Jesus pin."

Say what you will, if not for the rhinestone Jesus pin, I could still be wandering around in the Atlanta airport. Perhaps I have watched too many episodes of *Touched by an Angel!*[3]

CHAPTER XXXVII

Yeah, But Not Today!

n 1995, a spot on my lung was discovered. After much testing it was determined I should have surgery. I was overcome with fear and anxiety, as I tend to get melodramatic at times. Perhaps it is my Russian heritage. I was sure I was going to die. When I thought of my family and how they would miss me, I wept uncontrollably.

I knew all the right Scriptures and I had used them many times to console others going through a crisis, but somehow they brought me no consolation. One day, while reading the Bible, I came across II Timothy 1:7: "For God has not given us a spirit of fear, but of power, and of love, and of a sound mind."

It suddenly dawned on me that the immense fear I was experiencing was not appropriate to my circumstances. This fear was from Satan, the Enemy.

The next day as I prayed, God showed me that the fear had become a mountain in my life overshadowing His grace. I felt a great surge of faith rise up in me and I was able to pray for the mountain to be moved.

Little by little, the awful fear and anxiety left me, and my peace returned. By the time I went for surgery I was full of peace, able to experience God's all sufficient grace.

The spot did turn out to be lung cancer; however, it was very contained. Though a lobe of my lung was removed I miraculously did not need chemotherapy or radiation. It has now been five years since that surgery and my doctor has proclaimed me cured. Praise God!

I consider myself very fortunate that my cancer was in the early stages when discovered. I had no pain or other symptoms. It was discovered when my doctor thought I might have pneumonia during a bout of the flu. How fortunate I was! If that spot had not been not discovered until I had symptoms, I might not be alive today.

I haven't quite figured out the Christian dichotomy: we want to go to heaven, but we pray to be healed. I think my daughter Elena summed it up well when she was five years old. We were on an amusement park ride that stopped in mid-air. She cried, "Mommy, I'm so scared!"

We had just come back from Word of Life camp where we both had asked Jesus to be our Lord. I replied, "Honey, if we should fall and die we will be with Jesus. Don't you want to go to heaven?"

She replied, "Yeah, but not today!"

I consider myself to be a very healthy person, yet as I look back I see several major surgeries in the past such as gallbladder, hysterectomy, knee replacement and the lung cancer. I guess I am what you might call a "high maintenance model." I suffered a great deal of pain with each surgery, but it drove me further into God's arms, which is where I want to be. So I am grateful for them. I am also grateful that I recover quickly once I start to heal. God has been more than gracious to me.

Psalm 34:19 says, "Many are the troubles of the righteous, but the Lord delivers him from them all."

CHAPTER XXXVIII

Teeth Are Like Stars
That Come Out at Night

There is an old wives' tale that says, "For every child born, you lose a tooth." Well, this old wife can attest to this. By the time I was fifty I needed full dentures. I could not afford to go the root canal and cap route, so full dentures was my fate. After several fittings, which was a torturous ordeal of having my mouth filled with what seemed like cement, the day finally arrived for the unveiling of my new teeth.

The dentist slipped them into my mouth and handed me a mirror. His proud smile looked like he had just unveiled a masterpiece. What I saw in the mirror was someone, resembling me, with a weird mouthful of big, white teeth. The dentist, sensing my hesitancy to delight in my new look, called in his assistants. As though it had been rehearsed, they "Oohed and aahed." In view of their approval, perhaps I didn't look so weird after all.

My first stop after leaving the office was the drugstore where my youngest daughter worked. I found her busily stocking shelves. I approached her with a nonchalant, "Hi, Elena," as I flashed her my new, toothy smile.

She immediately broke into hysterical laughter. I was a little puzzled by her reaction. Especially after the appreciative reception my teeth had received at the dental office.

My next stop was to my home. My twenty-one year old, cynical, son greeted me. He did not laugh. Instead he asked, "Why do you have teeth like the *Alien*?"

By this time my confidence was really shaken. I decided to pay a visit and introduce my new teeth to my daughter, Rosie, who was my confidante. She did not think I had alien teeth. But, it was hard to know what she was thinking because she was laughing so hard she was crying.

This was not the best day of my life. Something was obviously wrong. I couldn't help but wonder if the people who worked at the dental office were sincere in their compliments or if their positive reaction was the standard line which they rehearsed on Wednesdays when the dental office was closed.

It was hard to synchronize those teeth. Sometimes when I opened my mouth, the teeth wouldn't follow suit. I felt like a ventriloquist. My lips moved but my teeth stayed closed. Eventually I discovered the miracle of denture adhesive. I may not be able to chomp the kernels off an ear of corn, or bite into a big juicy apple like they show on TV when they advertise those dental products, but ice cream and chocolate cake are, well ... a piece of cake for me.

One summer night, while I was playing miniature golf with three of the children, sans dental adhesive, something made me sneeze—a really big sneeze. Out flew my upper dentures. After what seemed like an eternity they landed at the feet of the man playing in front of us as he was getting ready to take his turn. From the look on his face, he seemed to think his golf ball had turned into teeth that were going to bite him! I lurched forward, fell to the ground and covered those dentures with my body. After recovering them, I forfeited the game. Those teeth earned me enormous mileage on the laugh meter and that event goes down in my history as My Most Embarrassing Moment!

Chapter XXXIX

It Ain't Over Till It's Over

I can hardly believe I have officially become a septuagenarian. It doesn't seem possible that I am becoming a little, old lady. I have actually shrunk two inches from my former 5'6".

Thanks to my daughter, Elena, I have a fashionable haircut and most of the time I look presentable. However, sometimes when I look in the mirror my grandmother is staring back at me. I am a little (all right, a lot) overweight. But, inside, there is a slim person that I have hopes will spring forth some day.

In spite of how I look on the outside I am young and alive on the inside. I may not dance in the aisles anymore, but within me I am still dancing.

I thank the Lord for the good times and the bad that have caused me to grow and become strong. I see a similarity between the flowers of the field and me. Having weathered all types of climate and other challenges, I am able to withstand the winds and storms of life. I am not of the variety which grow and bloom wonderfully in the greenhouse but cannot survive the harsh winds and storms outdoors.

I look forward to the future because I believe the best is yet to come. God doesn't promise us a rose garden. He promises us life and all that it entails. He also promises that He will be with us through the hard times.

I have known the hurt that alcohol, drug abuse and divorce can cause a family. As I used to tell my son, Tom, when he was a boy complaining about the injustices in life, "There is no paradise on earth." He sometimes reminds me of that now. Yet, sometimes—on good days—it comes pretty close to paradise.

By far, the most meaningful accomplishment in my life is being a mother. I am grateful to have been blessed with six sons and six daughters. Nothing even comes close to that honor. If I could get on a loudspeaker and broadcast to the parents of the world, I would tell them how precious are the lives with which God has entrusted them. I would remind them that their children do not belong to them, they belong to God. He has entrusted to parents the sacred responsibility to raise our children for Him. I would say, "Be willing to sacrifice and lay down your life and your wants for your children. Make their spiritual, emotional and physical welfare your top priority."

I have poured my life into my children, doing the best I could. I acknowledge that I have been far from a perfect parent. My hope is that they will live by the right principles I have taught them and forgive my mistakes. I pray they will pass on the things I did right to their children, and the cycle of love will go on for generations. I take solace in knowing that they have a heavenly parent who loves them perfectly. He makes no mistakes and He is able to heal any hurts I have caused.

My children are grown now and raising their children. I am so proud of the men and women they are today. Besides being my children, they are my friends. They have given us twenty-five grandchildren with another on the way. I have been blessed to see two of the grandchildren marry, and two grandchildren serving the Lord on the mission fields.

If I could live my life over would I marry at fifteen? Would I have twelve children? I know it was God's plan for us to marry when we did even though I was so young. I was definitely headed in the wrong direction and He used Sal to rescue me. After more than fifty years of marriage, I love my husband more than ever and I know he loves me.

I would do it again. Sal says, "Our marriage is like a strong, sturdy ship that has been able to withstand the storms and almost engulfing waves in the sea of matrimony." I believe he is right.

In response to the beautician who groaned, "You would have to be crazy to have twelve children," I would reply, "If it could be this bunch, I would have to be crazy not to!" However, we didn't plan to have twelve children. We would never be that courageous. But there is not one of these beautiful children we could do without. I know I could not have planned to have six sons and six daughters.

It took everything we had to raise our family, but every great accomplishment takes sacrifice and commitment. The joy we have reaped from our children is far exceeds the effort it took.

Six weeks ago I had a routine mammogram (sounds like a breast telegram doesn't it?). They immediately repeated it in another position. Then they did an ultrasound. Then the radiologist came out after that with the films. He showed me a black streak and said, "This must come out."

Within a few days I heard from my gynecologist and primary care physician who confirmed that the large mass in my breast had to be removed. They told me to quickly see the surgeon, which I did. Prepared for very bad news, I endured the surgeon's exam. She examined me and said, "After looking at your films I came in prepared to tell you that you have a large, cancerous mass, but I don't feel anything that the films show." To be on the safe side Dr. McManus scheduled a biopsy. Just to be sure she took a large section of breast tissue to be examined for any malignancy.

Praise the Lord! There was no cancer! However the scar from the biopsy did not heal well. It became very infected and had to be drained several times. The scar is quite unseemly. I am afraid I will never be able to prosper in a career as a topless dancer!

Last week while I was showering I asked the Lord, "Why this ugly scar?" He replied, "Every time you look at the scar, be reminded of my grace to you when I healed you of the cancer everyone thought the films showed.

As I finish writing my story, I realize this has been a time of reflection and gratitude for my life. I am in awe of the grace God has so lavishly poured out on us as a family. I don't know what tomorrow holds, but I do know who holds tomorrow; and I have peace. I pray the Lord will give me many more days to tell of His love and faithfulness. I want to finish my race strong.

I want to be able to say to the Lord, "I have fought a good fight, I have finished my course, I have kept the faith" (II Timothy 4:7).

Until then, in the words of baseball great, Yogi Berra, "It ain't over till it's over."

And, it ain't over, yet. So I say to you, go and live the life God has given you to His glory!

Endnotes

1. Tom Brokaw, *The Greatest Generation* (New York: Random House, Inc., 1998).

2. Dr. Larry Crabb, *The Marriage Builder: A Blueprint for Couples and Counselors* (Grand Rapids: Zondervan, 1992).

3. *Touched By An Angel* (New York: CBS Productions in association with Moon Water Productions, Inc.).